THE FAITH ONCE DELIVERED

In 2 Thessalonians 2:10 the Bible says that those "who are perishing" do so "because they refused to love the truth and so be saved." By contrast, those who are saved by Christ, that is, true Christians, are characterized as those who do love the truth of God. One of the greatest evidences of loving the truth is a lifelong, unquenchable desire to learn it. Since the earliest days of the church, catechizing has been one of the primary means Christians have used to learn the truth they love. The most useful catechisms don't just provide questions and answers—they also explain the answers. *The Faith Once Delivered* is one such catechism. It can be used with children or adults, in the home or in a group setting. Anyone who teaches it will find it an accessible, practical resource. Anyone who learns it will be blessed.

DONALD S. WHITNEY, professor of biblical spirituality and associate dean for the School of Theology, The Southern Baptist Theological Seminary, Louisville, Kentucky, USA; author of *Spiritual Disciplines for the Christian Life, Praying the Bible* and *Family Worship*

The idea of a Baptist catechism sounds strange to most Baptists, but that illustrates the pervasive ignorance of church history in our churches. In this very useful book, Craig Carter not only calls us back to *catechesis*, but also provides a catechism and its exposition to provide a way to do it. The people of God are more interested in thinking seriously about their faith than pastors often realize, and what is required is robust theology communicated in a form that is clear and engaging. Craig Carter has been doing that in his church, and this book is the fruit of that labour. I anticipate that I will use this in my church, and I commend it to others.

STANLEY K. FOWLER, professor of theological studies, Heritage College & Seminary, Cambridge, Ontario

---

The Faith Once Delivered is a wonderful tool to help the church equip new believers and those wanting to grow in their understanding of basic Christianity. Craig has put together an evangelical catechism that is both robust theologically and centred on the gospel. In these days of growing biblical and theological ignorance, such a work is so needed for equipping the body of Christ. It is uniquely both orthodox and missionally focused. I would highly recommend this excellent tool to church leaders.

RICK BUCK, lead pastor, Emmanuel Barrie, Barrie, Ontario

Dr. Craig Carter has ably shown the history of, and the needed revival of, both catechism and creed for the twenty-first century evangelical church. But he goes beyond that and gives the church a practical and usable tool for teaching the essential biblical and theological truths of the evangelical faith, and for the actual practice of catechism. While the catechism Carter develops is distinctly Baptist in its view of the mode and theology of baptism in particular, and at times has somewhat of a polemical feel, the book has great potential to serve the wider evangelical church in the increasingly important and needed domain of biblical and theological education in the local church.

DAVE BARKER, professor of pastoral studies & Old Testament, Heritage College & Seminary, Cambridge, Ontario

The vital importance of a sound catechism in teaching and preserving right doctrine cannot be overstated. This is what makes this book by Craig A. Carter so important to your Christian faith. Here is a faithful exposition of the Apostles' Creed, presented in a catechism format, that is thoroughly biblical, theologically accurate and yet practically relevant. You will do well to explore the truths contained in these pages, internalize them into your daily life and pass them down to the next generation.

STEVEN J. LAWSON, president, OnePassion Ministries, Dallas, Texas, USA

Dr. Carter has given a great gift to the church—a publication from a serious scholar and seasoned pastoral leader that is both accessible and weighty, designed to assist in the intentional spiritual formation of the people of God. This book emerges from many years of formal academic study and several decades of providing both quality instruction in the academy and leadership and teaching in the trenches of local church ministry. I highly commend this resource to pastors and all others involved in the teaching ministry of their church who want to take people deeper in their knowledge and practice of their faith.

BRUCE FAWCETT, president and vice chancellor, Crandall University, Moncton, New Brunswick

"In an age of secularism and relativism, the catechism is a symbol of radical discipleship." What a remarkable description of the promise of catechetical instruction: to produce followers of the Lord Jesus who are totally committed to him and to his Kingdom, to its principles and to its values. Having long been convinced of the value of using catechisms for teaching the Christian faith, I was thrilled to see a while ago the *Westney Catechism*, drawn up by Professor Carter as an instructional tool in his local church in Ajax, Ontario. It is equally thrilling to now see this exposition of the *Westney Catechism*. May it get a much-needed wide audience beyond Professor Carter's local church.

MICHAEL A.G. HAYKIN, professor of church history and biblical spirituality and director of The Andrew Fuller Center for Baptist Studies, The Southern Baptist Theological Seminary, Louisville, Kentucky, USA

This needed and practical book is a very helpful tool for every pastor and Christian leader who strives to see the body of Christ built up, progressing toward unity in the faith and growing up in the knowledge and fullness of Christ. The author's justification for the recovery of the time-honoured practice of *catechesis* is beautifully supported by this biblically sound, balanced and accessible guide to the essentials of Christian faith. Wisely and judiciously written, this book anticipates the questions of the contemporary audience well, providing substantial yet accessible answers, complete with down-to-earth illustrations and examples. I highly recommend this important church-wide discipleship tool.

DALE DAWSON, lead pastor, Uxbridge Baptist Church, Uxbridge, Ontario

Craig Carter's *The Faith Once Delivered* is an excellent primer of Christian theology and practice for all followers of Christ in general, and for new believers in particular. It covers all the basic teachings and practices that every church member should know and implement based on the Ten Commandments and the Lord's prayer including emphases on baptism, Lord's Supper and mission. There are three things I deeply appreciate about Craig's book. The first is that it is structured around a catechism that he has developed at his church. This enables the reader, as they read the book and memorize the catechism, to remember these basic teachings throughout their lives. Second, the structure flows along a biblical theological model of creation, fall and redemption, with Christ as the central figure in the biblical story. This helps the reader see that the gospel is central to scripture, their lives and the life of the church. And third, Craig brings his years of experience as a theologian and pastor to his articulation of the faith. This is quite evident from his simple and yet theologically thoughtful presentation of the church's teachings and practice that all believers should and need to embrace. I highly recommend this book to pastors to use for a new members class (13 week structure) or for adult or young adult Bible studies. This would even be a good refresher for church boards to read, study and discuss at the beginning of their meetings. Very well done, Craig, and thanks for this very useful tool for helping make disciples in the church.

BARRY HOWSON, PhD, academic dean, Heritage College & Seminary, Cambridge, Ontario

---

Keeping the main things the main thing is always a challenge in the church and our personal lives these days. If evangelism, discipleship and good doctrine are three legs of that stool then Dr. Carter has provided the basics for stability and grounding. Using Scripture and the Apostles' Creed, and adding the catechism methodology, he provides a sound base and exposure to the necessary basics as a resource for personal, small group or large church study sessions. I recommend this book.

JACK HANNAH, community pastor, Westney Heights Baptist Church, Ajax, Ontario

THE FAITH
ONCE DELIVERED

An introduction
to the basics of the
Christian faith

An exposition of the Westney Catechism

Craig A. Carter

joshua
press

For the people of
Westney Heights Baptist Church,
who love to study the Word of Truth,
and for
Pastor Jack Hannah,
who gave me the opportunity to minister
at Westney ten years ago and has been
a constant encouragement ever since.

I thank my God in all my remembrance of you,
always in every prayer of mine for you all
making my prayer with joy,
because of your partnership in the gospel
from the first day until now.
(Philippians 1:3–5)

p r e s s

www.joshuapress.com

Published by
Joshua Press Inc., Kitchener, Ontario, Canada
Distributed by
Sola Scriptura Ministries International
www.sola-scriptura.ca

First published 2018

Cover and book design by Janice Van Eck

The publication of this book was made possible by the generous support of The Ross-Shire Foundation.

Library and Archives Canada Cataloguing in Publication

Carter, Craig, 1956-, author
    The faith once delivered : an introduction to the basics
of the Christian faith—an exposition of the Westney catechism
/ Craig A. Carter.

Includes bibliographical references.
Issued in print and electronic formats.
ISBN 978-1-894400-87-9 (softcover).—ISBN 978-1-894400-88-6
(HTML).—ISBN 978-1-894400-89-3 (PDF)

    1. Faith. I. Title.

BV4637.C349 2018   234'.23   C2018-901467-9
                                            C2018-901468-7

Contents

Preface

The primary purpose of this book is to introduce the reader to the basics of the Christian faith through an exposition of the Westney Catechism (see the Appendix for the complete catechism). The use of *catechesis* as a way of grounding believers in the faith needs to be revived in our day, and the aim of this book is to make a contribution to that important effort.

Those who teach the catechism to others—whether they be children or adults—will find this book helpful in expanding on the succinct answers given in the catechism. The book follows the outline of the seven parts of the catechism in thirteen chapters. The catechism can be taught in seven or thirteen class sessions in Sunday School or in a small group format. Each chapter closes with "Questions for reflection" which can be used as a guide for discussion.

It is my hope this book can be used in other ways as well. Perhaps for private study by someone wanting to learn or review the basics of the historic Christian faith in its evangelical, Protestant and baptistic form. It could also form the basis of a sermon series for pastors desiring to teach doctrine to their congregation in a systematic manner. It could also be used as a teacher's resource or as something to be read by candidates for baptism and/or church membership. Pastors may wish to have their deacons or elders read it to ensure their leadership is on the same page doctrinally.

This book has grown out of my teaching and preaching ministry at Westney Heights Baptist Church, Ajax, Ontario, over the past decade. This multi-ethnic church with approximately 500 people in attendance on a

Sunday morning comprises people from all over the world who have come to the Greater Toronto Area. I have preached sermon series' on the Ten Commandments, the Lord's Prayer, Baptism and the Lord's Supper, and I have preached sermons on the Great Commandment and the Great Commission. I also taught the Apostles' Creed in an adult Sunday School class over a thirteen-week period. We often speak of church growth as meaning more than simply numerical growth, and in teaching this material God has blessed us with a great deal of spiritual growth. For example, some people testified the series on baptism was used by God to convict them of their need to be baptized. Others have gained a new appreciation of the importance of world missions, while still others have come to understand the need for personal Bible study in their lives. God has used this teaching at Westney, and my prayer is that he would continue to use it in book form.

In these days of confusion and doctrinal vagueness, it is my hope that many more churches will discover the joy of clear convictions and biblical truth. May this book contribute to making this hope a reality.

Acknowledgements

I would like to acknowledge the help of many people in producing this book. My wife Bonnie has been a true partner in the work of ministry for over forty years. She is a major influence on everything I write and, indeed, my ability to get any writing done at all. I am grateful to God for her. I also want to thank Pastor Don Symons for working with me on the catechism on which this book is based. I am also grateful to my daughter, Rebecca, for doing the proofreading.

The material in this book has been preached or taught at Westney Heights Baptist Church over the past ten years as I have served as theologian-in-residence. Westney is no ordinary church. It is a fellowship of ethnically diverse people from every part of the world, with dozens of mother tongues—united by their living faith in Jesus Christ. I have never been part of a fellowship so devoted to the serious study of God's Word. What a privilege it is to minister in this context!

The Bible-loving character of the church was shaped by the founding pastor, Rev. Jim Rendle, who still serves on the pastoral staff part-time, more than a quarter century after founding the church. It was nurtured by the second pastor, Rev. Jack Hannah, who still serves on staff as well. Our current senior pastor, Rev. Don Symons, has continued to develop the church's love for Scriptural teaching and has been a great encouragement to me by providing opportunities for using my gifts in teaching and preaching for the common good of the body. All three of these gifted men have been very encouraging to me as I have ministered at Westney over the past decade.

1

Why do we need a catechism?

"In an age of secularism and relativism, the catechism is a symbol of radical discipleship."

INTRODUCTION:
WHAT DOES A CHRISTIAN NEED TO BELIEVE?

The universal church of Jesus Christ cannot be destroyed, but local churches can be, and have been, destroyed at various times in church history. The fact that a certain country was highly Christianized for a long period of time does not mean that the church in that country necessarily will last indefinitely. Any local church including ours is two or three generations away from extinction at any given moment in time.

We can see the truth of this statement in the history of the church. The great church father, Augustine of Hippo, was a bishop, theologian and apologist. He was the greatest Christian thinker of the fifth century and the most influential theologian during the next thousand years of Christendom. But he died in 430 A.D. with the barbarians literally at the gates of his city, and shortly after his death the city was conquered and the Christian church in North Africa was greatly weakened. Within 200 years of Augustine's death, the North African church was destroyed by invading Muslim armies and, between A.D. 647 and 709, Christianity gradually died out in North Africa. From the fall of the Roman Empire in the fifth century to the early Middle Ages, however, Europe was gradually evangelized and Europe became the main stronghold of the Christian faith for a millennium. But today, Christianity is dying out in Europe, and the churches of Europe are in the minority with a decreasing amount of cultural influence. The centre of world Christianity has shifted to North America, yet Christianity is in retreat here too. The main areas of growth for the church during the twentieth century were sub-Saharan Africa and China. Individual, local churches rise and fall and never stand still; Christianity is always either advancing or declining. The church is either growing or declining.

The reasons why local and national churches decline and eventually become extinct are complex. But one thing we can say for sure is that one extremely important factor is a loss of a firm grasp of sound doctrine. This is why the apostle Paul is so insistent in his letters to Timothy and Titus that they make it a priority to teach sound doctrine. Paul writes to Timothy:

> You then, my child, be strengthened by the grace that is in Christ Jesus, and what you have heard from me in the presence of many witnesses entrust to faithful men, who will be able to teach others also (2 Timothy 2:1–2).

This is Timothy's top priority: teach sound doctrine so that the gospel can be passed on from one generation to the next. Later in the letter, Paul urges Timothy to preach and teach sound doctrine as a matter of urgency:

> I charge you in the presence of God and of Christ Jesus, who is to judge the living and the dead, and by his appearing and his kingdom: preach the word; be ready in season and out of season; reprove, rebuke, and exhort, with complete patience and teaching (2 Timothy 4:1–2).

Why is there such urgency about this task? Paul explains in the next two verses:

> For the time is coming when people will not endure sound teaching, but having itching ears they will accumulate for themselves teachers to suit their own passions, and will turn away from listening to the truth and wander off into myths (2 Timothy 4:3–4).

Paul writes to Titus specifically exhorting him to "teach what accords with sound doctrine" (Titus 2:1). In his last speech to the Ephesian elders

Paul warns them that after he is gone:

> fierce wolves will come in among you, not sparing the flock; and from among your own selves will arise men speaking twisted things, to draw away the disciples after them (Acts 20:29–30).

The battle for sound doctrine in the church is a form of spiritual warfare in which the eternal destiny of souls is at stake. When a church dies, it is not merely the death of an institution. It means that people have turned away from Christ into damnation and hopelessness and others have lost the opportunity to hear the gospel and be saved. Paul is passionate about doctrine because he is passionate about precious human beings and their eternal destiny. But it is not just Paul who speaks this way; all the New Testament apostolic writers share the same concern.

Along the same lines, Jude writes:

> I found it necessary to write appealing to you to contend for the faith that was once for all delivered to the saints (Jude 3).

John shows a similar concern for sound doctrine in his first letter when he writes:

> Beloved, do not believe every spirit, but test the spirits to see whether they are from God, for many false prophets have gone out into the world (1 John 4:1).

He then goes on to give a doctrinal test to distinguish true from false teachers:

> By this you know the Spirit of God: every spirit that confesses that Jesus Christ has come in the flesh is from God, and every spirit that does not confess Jesus is not from God. This is the spirit of the antichrist, which you heard was coming and now is in the world already (1 John 4:2–3).

False doctrine is a mark of the antichrist. The wolves Paul spoke of are not just random predators—they are agents or tools of the antichrist, who is, himself, the tool of dark spiritual forces greater than he. The apostle Peter identifies the ultimate source of false doctrine when he warns his readers,

> Your adversary the devil prowls around like a roaring lion, seeking someone to devour (1 Peter 5:8).

Paul says to preach and teach. Jude says to contend earnestly. John says to test the spirits. Peter urges us to resist the devil. Why do we need a catechism? It is a weapon in a spiritual battle the church is called to fight until the return of Christ. The issue is the salvation of souls, the thwarting of the evil powers and the survival of the church in the teeth of foes who would infiltrate, deceive and ultimately destroy her out of hatred for the God she worships and the gospel she declares before the watching world.

There is never any guarantee that the congregation will listen to the Word, but the preacher must preach no matter what. The preaching and teaching ministry of the church is fundamental to the spiritual health and life of the local church. This is why the ministry of *catechesis* is so important; it mobilizes Christians in support of a faithful pulpit ministry so that it is not just one soldier in the battle but the entire army. We must teach the faith to new members, the children of the church and to all who assemble week by week for the preaching of the gospel. Without sound doctrine, the church cannot stand when the winds of heresy and persecution blow against it. This is why John Calvin famously said that the church cannot survive without *catechesis*.[1]

The stakes are high: Will the Christian church survive two more generations and hand on the gospel faithfully? This is the question all of us must be concerned with as we ponder the situation in the contemporary world. People today worry about a lot of things: ecological disaster, the spectre of nuclear war, the state of the economy, the threat of terrorism, the culture of death that is tightening its grip on the Western world, and so on. But whether the gospel survives is infinitely more important than all these issues combined, because it concerns the only hope for the world. Will the church preserve the gospel, preach the gospel and hand on the gospel to the next generation of believers? Or will the church distort the gospel, forget the gospel and let it disappear from human history?

Of course, we believe in the sovereignty of God and the inevitability of his promises. We know that the gospel will not disappear from the earth until the full number of the elect is gathered in from every tribe and nation. But we also know that the gospel has virtually disappeared from certain geographical areas of the world. What we should be concerned with is what will happen to the church in North America. We are responsible for our own culture and for our own church.

Will we pass on the faith to our children and to future generations or will we be the link in the chain that fails to hold? God's providence is mysterious, and we do not see the future as he does. All we can do is look around us at our times and try to understand them on the basis of what we know of the

---

[1] As quoted in J.I. Packer and Gary A. Parrett, *Grounded in the Gospel: Building Believers the Old-Fashioned Way* (Grand Rapids: Baker Books, 2010), 51.

history of the church and the teaching of Scripture. As we look at the church in North America today, the picture is troubling. Cultural trends like relativism, atheism and secularism are working against us. We are in a struggle for the souls of our children. It is time to begin to take our faith more seriously and to make sure that we are doing the job Christ entrusted to us as his church.

As parents, we want our children to grow up and embrace faith in Christ themselves. As pastors and deacons, we want the members of our church to be protected from heresy and firmly rooted in Christ. Part of the duty of pastors and parents is to teach those who have been entrusted to our care the basics of the faith. But what, exactly, does that entail? As church members, we want to ensure that our church does not go off the rails like so many churches today have done. We want to ensure that we continue to believe the biblical, orthodox faith.

What are the key beliefs of Christian orthodoxy? As Christians, we want to obey Jesus Christ who commanded the church to evangelize and to teach converts all he commanded. How do we know when we have taught them the basics of Christian faith adequately?

The question: "What do Christians need to believe?" is too broad. We need to break it down into three sub-questions:

1. What do you need to know in order to be *saved*?
2. What do you need to know in order to *serve* the Lord?
3. What do you need to know in order to *guard* the gospel?

The goal of this catechism is to go beyond the basics of what one needs to know in order to be saved. What one needs to believe in order to become a Christian is minimal:

1. We must believe that God exists and that he is a holy and just God whose wrath is directed against all sin.
2. We must believe that we are sinners who are separated from him and under his wrath because of our disobedience and rebellion.
3. We must believe that God sent his only Son, Jesus Christ, to die on the cross in order to pay the penalty for our sin.
4. Then we must repent of our sins, believe the gospel, and put our trust in Jesus Christ alone as our only hope of salvation, thus acknowledging him as our Lord and Saviour.

When a person knows the first three of these things and then repents, believes and trusts as described above, then he or she is saved. A child can grasp this much, although the profundity of these truths is too great for any human being to comprehend fully even after a lifetime of study. Once a person does grasp these basics of the gospel, however, he or she needs to be instructed more fully in the Christian faith, baptized and enrolled as a member of a local church. Just as a newborn baby has passed a significant milestone by being born healthy and safe, newborn Christians need to eat, drink, exercise, sleep and grow up.

Birth is the end of the journey through the birth canal, but it is merely the beginning of the journey through life! For the rest of one's life, one needs to grow spiritually by constantly learning more about what it means to be a Christian. Bible study should be a regular part of every Christian's life on a permanent basis. The catechism is a foundation for a lifetime of Bible study. Every Christian should study and digest the teachings in it. We need to establish a baseline for our church so that we can assume that all members of our church understand and believe what the catechism covers. Many Christians will go much deeper, but hopefully none will fail to go this far.

Some of us will be called to go further in our studies. Many people in evangelical churches either have gone to a Bible college or seminary or are enrolled in one at this very moment. In his letters to Timothy, we see how the apostle Paul stressed with great urgency the importance of watching over the flock and guarding the gospel so it could be handed down intact from one generation to the next. Some of us will be called to be shepherds of the flock and guardians of the gospel like Timothy. Those individuals will need further education at a Bible college or seminary.

In our study of the catechism we are aiming at the middle range: *more* than what one needs to know in order to be a born-again Christian and *less* than what a person needs to know in order to be the senior pastor of a church. We are focused on what the ordinary church member needs to know in order to serve as a parent, a Sunday school teacher, a deacon or a Bible study group leader.

Some people might question why we need to call it a *catechism*. That word conjures up visions of the Roman Catholic Church for some people, and it doesn't sound very Baptist. But no denomination has a monopoly on biblical words. Non-Baptist churches practice baptism and non-Pentecostal churches emphasize the reality of Pentecost. The Christian Reformed churches are not the only reformed churches in the world; nor are they claiming to be the only Christians. Likewise, Roman Catholics are not the only ones who claim to be part of the catholic or universal church. So we should not shy away from using a biblical word to describe a church ministry just because other denominations use it. And, as we shall see, the Bible itself speaks of *catechesis*. But what, exactly, is a catechism? What is the nature of the problem such a tool helps to address? The best way to answer this question is to turn to Scripture.

I. *CATECHESIS* IN THE BIBLE

The word *katecheo* is used in the New Testament numerous times, and it means "teaching" or "instruction" in general. However, even in the New Testament itself, there is the beginning of a more specific usage in which this word becomes a technical term referring to the communication of basic Christian knowledge to new converts.[2]

For example, Luke writes to Theophilus that he has written a well-researched account of the life and works of Jesus "that you may have certainty concerning the things you have been taught (*katecho*)" (Luke 1:3–4). If Theophilus was a believer already, then the word *katecheo* here may refer to the formal instruction he received before baptism. As a Greek, Theophilus would not have had the biblical teaching that those brought up in a Jewish family would have had, so he would have been in need of *catechesis* prior to baptism. On the other hand, if Theophilus was not yet a believer, or not yet baptized, then Luke's Gospel could be regarded as an elaboration on the basic instruction given to a seeker or candidate for baptism. The Gospel of Luke is not a work of apologetics, but of instruction, and may have been written originally for the purpose of being used in *catechesis* or for taking new Christians beyond the basics of *catechesis*.

Paul writes, "the one who is taught the word must share all good things with the one who teaches" (Galatians 6:6). If we simply keep the Greek words in the English translation we could translate this as: "The *catechumen* must share all good things with the *catechist*."

The *catechumen* is the one being taught. The *catechist* is the instructor. The *catechesis* is the process of teaching new converts and preparing them for baptism. The *catechism* is the written summary of the faith in question and answer format that is used in this process of teaching. All four forms of this word are transliterations of the Greek words used in the New Testament.

Soon after the close of the New Testament canon, the office of "catechist" became a widespread fixture in the early church. As the church moved out of the Jewish milieu and into the pagan, Greco-Roman world, it began to evangelize people with no knowledge of the Hebrew Scriptures and no understanding of basic theological concepts such as creation and sin. Baptizing such people without a period of basic instruction in the Christian faith seemed irresponsible, so *catechesis* in preparation for baptism became an essential part of the church's ministry.

But the basic idea of *catechesis* is found already in the Old Testament. For example, in Deuteronomy we read:

---

[2] Packer & Parrett, *Grounded in the Gospel*, 38.

> Hear, O Israel: The LORD our God, the LORD is one. You shall love the LORD your God with all your heart and with all your soul and with all your might. And these words that I command you today shall be on your heart. You shall teach them diligently to your children, and shall talk of them when you sit in your house, and when you walk by the way, and when you lie down, and when you rise. You shall bind them as a sign on your hand, and they shall be as frontlets between your eyes. You shall write them on the doorposts of your house and on your gates (Deuteronomy 6:4–9).

This is known as the *Shema*, the creed of Israel: "Hear, O Israel: The LORD our God, the LORD is one." This is a basic affirmation of the uniqueness of God. There is only one true God, and he demands Israel's full loyalty and devotion. Therefore, verse 5 continues: "You shall love the LORD your God with all your heart and with all your soul and with all your might." In verses 6–9 we find that God commands the Israelites to teach these words diligently to their children. By the way, the *Shema* is found in chapter 6 of Deuteronomy, which follows the second listing of the Ten Commandments, which we see in chapter 5.

The book of Deuteronomy is set on the plains of Moab and consists of Moses giving his last exhortations to the people of Israel just before they enter the Promised Land under Joshua. Moses gives the Ten Commandments a second time after the forty years of wandering in the wilderness and then, in chapter six, he stresses the importance of keeping these commands in the pagan environment of Canaan. He tells Israel that they will have long life and blessing in the land providing that they put God first, remember his words and obey his commands. Otherwise they will experience God's wrath and ultimately disaster.

Passing on the basics of the faith from one generation to the next is the most important thing we have to do as the people of God. This is true in the Old Testament and also in the New Testament, as we saw at the beginning of this chapter. Now we need to take a quick glance at the importance of *catechesis* in church history.

II. *CATECHESIS* IN CHURCH HISTORY

As the gospel moved from Jerusalem to Judea to Samaria to the ends of the earth, it moved from a Jewish context shaped by the Hebrew Scriptures to a pagan context in which religious confusion reigned and numerous mutually contradictory religions and philosophies competed with each other for the attention of people in the late Roman empire. The sheer number of pagan gods was overwhelming. Eastern religious sects were making inroads into the Western empire. Philosophers who rejected all popular religion and embraced a kind of monotheism were not uncommon.

The exalted ethical monotheism of the Jews proved to be attractive to many non-Jews as the beliefs of Jewish communities in cities around the Mediterranean basin became known. Although the Jews were a thorn in the side of the Roman emperors because of their obstinate refusal to participate in the pagan, polytheistic civil religion of the empire, many Romans nevertheless thought the Jewish religion was vastly superior to the crude paganism of Greco-Roman culture and the fantastic cults being imported from the East. For this reason, each Jewish synagogue had a circle of Gentile "God fearers" who gathered around the synagogue. These people accepted the biblical teaching that there is only one true God and the basic morality of the Ten Commandments as God's will for humanity. But they did not go all the way and convert to Judaism by accepting circumcision and the obligation to keep the entire Law of Moses.

The nucleus of many of the churches Paul founded on his missionary journeys came from the ranks of these God-fearing Gentiles. But soon these churches were engaged in outreach to complete pagans who lacked even the basics of monotheism and the moral law of God. They came from polytheistic backgrounds in which religion and ethical behaviour were completely unrelated. It soon became apparent that *catechesis* was no luxury in such a situation if the church wanted to avoid being paganized by converts who would bring paganism into the church. By the second century, we find that one of the main tasks of bishops and elders was *catechesis*.

The exact wording of the Apostles' Creed was finalized around the seventh century, but the basic creed in various local versions with minor variations goes back to the second century.[3] Thus, from very early in church history a version of the Apostles' Creed has been used in the preparation of candidates for baptism. In many instances, the person being baptized would have quoted the creed from memory as a confession of faith prior to baptism. The weeks leading up to baptism, which often took place at Easter, were spent preparing the candidates for baptism by teaching the creed. The importance of this task is seen in the fact that the chief pastor or bishop of a city or area often did the teaching personally.

During the early Middle Ages, the emphasis on catechism declined along with literacy and general educational standards. But by the high Middle Ages, when universities were founded, we see a great leap forward in education. This period saw the founding of the great teaching order, the Dominicans. The most famous Dominican of the medieval period was

---

[3] John H. Leith, *Creeds of the Churches: A Reader in Christian Doctrine from the Bible to the Present*, 2nd ed. (Louisville: Westminster John Knox Press, 1973), 22–24.

Thomas Aquinas, and a major part of his ministry was preparing friars to preach and teach the Bible to people and to engage in evangelism and apologetics. But the *catechesis* of the general church-going population was still at low ebb when the Reformation began in the sixteenth century.

All the Protestant Reformers strongly emphasized *catechesis*. John Calvin said: "Believe me...the Church of God will never be preserved without *catechesis*."[4] Martin Luther, John Calvin, Thomas Cranmer and many other Reformers even wrote catechisms for their own churches, some of which are still in use today. Wherever the Reformation spread, grammar schools to teach everyone to read were started; one of the primary motives for the emphasis on universal literacy and education was to enable everyone to read the Bible personally.

When the English Particular Baptists emerged out of the Church of England during the Puritan era in the seventeenth century, they also took *catechesis* seriously. The Westminster Confession of Faith of 1646 was a major statement of the Reformation in England, and it was produced along with a Larger and Shorter Catechism for use in teaching the faith to congregations. Baptists produced the First London Confessions in 1644 (second edition in 1646) in order to show that they were not Anabaptists and, in fact, shared most of the theology of the Westminster Confession. The only major differences were the articles on baptism and church government. A Second London Confession was drawn up in 1677 and then ratified by over 100 Baptist congregations in 1689, in continuation of the Reformed Baptist tradition. An English Baptist minister named Benjamin Keach was involved in drawing up a catechism that is today known as Keach's Catechism, to go with the Second London Confession.

Reformed Baptists in both England and America continued to uphold the theology of the London Confessions and to utilize catechisms in their ministry. For example, in 1753, the Philadelphia Association adopted the Second London Confession and Keach's Catechism for their own use.[5] In 1855 a young Charles Spurgeon edited a version of Keach's Catechism for the use of his congregation, the New Park Street Chapel. The most famous Baptist preacher of the nineteenth century wrote in the introduction:

> I am persuaded that the use of a good Catechism in all our families will be a great safeguard against the increasing errors of the times, and therefore I have compiled this little manual from the Westminster

---

[4] As quoted in Packer & Parrett, *Grounded in the Gospel*, 51.
[5] See the *Philadelphia Confession of Faith being the London Confession of Faith Adopted in 1742 by The Baptist Association with Scripture References and Keach's Catechism* (Sterling: G.A.M. Publications, 1981).

Assembly's and Baptist Catechisms, for the use of my own church and congregation. Those who use it in their families or classes must labour to explain the sense; but the words should be carefully learned by heart, for they will be understood better as years pass. May the Lord bless my dear friends and their families evermore."[6]

Throughout the first three centuries of Baptist life and witness, the catechism was an essential tool of Christian education. Regrettably, however, the twentieth century witnessed a drastic decline in the use of the catechism due to a number of historical factors, none of which were beneficial to the church. We need to revive this early church, Protestant Reformation and Baptist tool for inculcating a sound faith in our people.

III. *CATECHESIS* TODAY

Our age is marked by a decline in doctrinal preaching, Bible study and general Christian knowledge. The cultural environment of North America is growing more hostile to biblical Christianity with every passing year. Only a few years ago, many public schools educated children according to the morality of the Ten Commandments. Saying the Lord's Prayer in school was common, and Bible reading was not uncommon. Today, public school children are indoctrinated in the acceptability of sexual pleasure as a morally neutral, recreational activity. Christianity has been banished from the schools and the world of entertainment, with the result that the only way children will learn about God, the Bible and Christianity is from their families and in church. The change in just a few generations has been fundamental and far-reaching, and the church has been slow to react appropriately.

We increasingly live in a social environment more like that of the early church or the Reformation than like the nineteenth and early twentieth centuries. This means that we must take the task of educating children and adults more seriously than ever before. One way we can do this is to revive the ministry of *catechesis*.

John Calvin's statement that the Christian church could not survive without *catechesis* is a strong claim, but not one that can easily be refuted. In a situation such as the one we face, it becomes more obvious with each passing year that his view is the sober truth. A Baptist church is always two or three generations away from extinction. If there is not frequent revival and frequent evidence of the Holy Spirit regenerating individuals in the

---

[6] Charles H. Spurgeon, *A Catechism with Proofs* (Chapel Library, 2603 West Wright Sreet, Pensacola, FL 32505).

church, then the church will decline and die. And, if new Christians are not properly instructed in the faith, they will not become mature, contributing members, able to pass on the faith effectively to the next generation. *Catechesis* is not a luxury or an option but a necessity for the church today.

CONCLUSION:
A SURVIVAL PLAN FOR THE CHURCH IN A HOSTILE CULTURE

In such an environment as ours, we need three things:

1. Clarity
First, we need clarity about what we believe. We need to know what we believe, why we believe and how what we believe affects the way we ought to live. We cannot rely on Hollywood or public schools or general culture reflected in peer pressure to shape the beliefs and morals of our people. If we do, our people will become pagans. We need more than vague platitudes and clichés; we need a clear moral vision based on clear doctrinal beliefs. We need to know how what we believe differs from what the world around us believes and how to defend our convictions. Clarity is indispensable if we want to be faithful and pass on our faith to the next generation.

2. Catechesis
Second, if we are to have clarity, it will only come through knowledge that is clear and concise. We need to take the task of catechizing our children, new converts and those who seek membership in our church about the basics of the faith. We cannot assume that adults entering into our fellowship know the Bible or even basic doctrine. Sometimes we find new members who have been well taught, and we are glad when that is the case. But it would be foolish to presume it in all cases. When we baptize someone, we should make sure the candidate knows the basics of the faith first. And we need to follow the spirit of the commands in Deuteronomy 6 and teach our children constantly, clearly and with personal conviction.

3. Courage
Third, we need to have deep, personal convictions about what we believe. The time of testing is coming, in which those who are real Christians will be separated from those who are unwilling to suffer for the faith. Courage comes from clarity and *catechesis*; this is why we are introducing this teaching tool at this time. May God grant us the courage to believe, the courage to stand and the courage to continue in the gospel.

To believe in truth in a relativistic age is a political act that is deeply offensive to the powers that be. To speak the truth in such an age is an act of radical discipleship that brings persecution from worldly powers. To teach the truth to our children is an act of faith in a world that wants to wrest our children from us and rob them of faith in the gospel. To embrace a catechism is in itself an assertion that there is such a thing as truth, it can be summarized in words, and we are ready to let our "yes" be "yes" and our "no" be "no." In other words, we are ready to submit to the truth of the gospel and take our stand on it.

To some people, teaching and learning a catechism sounds boring and old fashioned. But to those who are on fire with the truth of God, it is like a long cold drink of water to a man in the desert and like a seven-course meal to the one who has not eaten in days. Loving doctrinal truth is one of the ways we love the One who said he was "the Truth." It is an act of radical discipleship.

Questions for reflection

1. Do you sense a growing gap between what you believe as a Christian and what the society around you believes? Can you give an example?

2. After the people of Israel entered the Promised Land, they did not keep the law and eventually were sent by God into exile in Babylon. What role do you think their failure to do *catechesis* played in this decline into judgement? Can you think of a biblical example where the lack of doctrinal knowledge hurt the people of God in the period when they were in the land?

3. What do you think would have happened if the early church had not catechized new Gentile converts? Is there any danger of similar things happening to us today?

4. Did you know that for most of Baptist history, Baptist churches used catechisms? Why do you think that practice declined in the twentieth century?

5. The author speaks of doing *catechesis* as an act of "radical discipleship." What do you think this means?

2

What is the problem that Christianity solves?

"Christianity is not a self-help message;
it is all about sin and salvation."

INTRODUCTION

Before we plunge into the first section of the catechism, we need to pause to take a quick bird's-eye overview of the whole catechism, which is divided into seven sections. Seven, by the way, in Jewish tradition, is the number of perfection and completion because God created the universe in six days and rested on the seventh day, having completed the work. The catechism is not complete in the sense of giving a comprehensive knowledge of Christian doctrine, but it does attempt to give a brief overview of the whole range of basic Christian beliefs. In this introductory chapter, we examine the first of the seven parts of the catechism. The next eleven chapters will expound the remaining six sections of the catechism.

The catechism's seven sections include:

1. The Great Commandment: What God requires of us (Q. 1–3)—
   Chapter 2
2. The Bible and the Apostles' Creed: Christian doctrine (Q. 4–27)—
   Chapters 3–7
3. Baptism: Christian conversion (Q. 28–35)—Chapter 8
4. The Ten Commandments: Christian ethics (Q. 36–55)—Chapters
   9–10
5. The Lord's Supper: Christian worship (Q. 56–63)—Chapter 11
6. The Lord's Prayer: Christian spirituality (Q. 64–77)—Chapter 12
7. The Great Commission: The mission of the church (Q. 78–84)—
   Chapter 13

One of the difficult decisions one has to make in constructing the catechism is where to put the Ten Commandments. On the one hand, it would make sense to place them at the beginning in order to follow the sequence of law and gospel so important to the Protestant Reformers. We first hear of the wrath of God against sin and disobedience and then we are prepared to hear the remedy for sin in the good news of the gospel. Without a consciousness of sin, the gospel means nothing to the person listening to the sermon.

On the other hand, the Reformers (John Calvin in particular) emphasized that the purpose of the law is threefold. Its first purpose is, of course, to convict us of our sin and make us long for the grace of the gospel. But it is also given, secondly, to provide a basis for civil society and to keep lawlessness in check so that the gospel can be preached in peace. And, thirdly, it also is given to help believers understand the shape of a holy life as a basis for Christian ethics. We can sum up the threefold purpose of the law as follows:

1. To convict sinners of sin
2. To provide a basis for civil law and public justice
3. To help believers understand what the holy life looks like

If we wish to stress only the first purpose, then the Ten Commandments should come at the beginning of the catechism, but if we wish to emphasize the second and third purposes as well, then they should come after the explanation of the gospel and conversion. We would then expound the Ten Commandments as a guide to holy living.

Jesus said in the Great Commission that we are supposed to teach new converts to observe "all that I have commanded you" (Matthew 28:20). So what did Jesus teach with regard to the law? First, we find that Jesus expounded the law as the shape of the redeemed life of the believer in the

Sermon on the Mount (Matthew 5–7). He largely assumed the civic purpose of the law as the basis for human government as any Jew in Israel would naturally do. But in the Sermon on the Mount he stressed that the Spirit-filled life of the New Testament believer is supposed to be a site where the *spiritual* intentions that God had in giving the Old Testament law would be fulfilled. Jeremiah spoke of a coming day when there would be a "new covenant" (Jeremiah 31:31) that would be written on the heart (v. 33) and, in the Lord's Supper, Jesus said that the cup is the "new covenant in my blood" (Luke 22:20). Jesus intended that those who believe in him and receive eternal life would be filled with the Holy Spirit and enabled to respond in heartfelt obedience to the deepest intentions God had in giving the law, and this new kind of life would be the essence of the Christian life.

Second, we find that when the Pharisees decided to ask Jesus a question to test him, a lawyer asked him: "Teacher, which is the great commandment in the Law?" (Matthew 22:36). Jesus answered by quoting two verses from the Torah that together summarized the Ten Commandments. Jesus quoted Deuteronomy 6:5, which focuses on the need to love God above all else, and Leviticus 19:18, which focuses on love for your neighbour (Matthew 22:37–40). The Ten Commandments represent the moral heart of the entire Torah, and these two commandments summarize the first and second tables of the law. In the Ten Commandments the first four focus on our duty to God and the last six on our duty to our neighbour.

In giving this answer, Jesus was saying that you cannot pinpoint a certain commandment that, providing you obey it, gives you license to ignore the rest of the law. If you try to love God, but neglect your neighbour, then *all* your worship is unacceptable to God. But if you try to love your neighbour while ignoring your religious duties to God, that is mere humanism and therefore false religion. Jesus is emphasizing the necessity of total obedience to the will of God as expressed in the entire law, including the intentions for which the law was given, and not merely external, formal obedience. Jesus' answer in Matthew 22 is in total harmony with his teaching in Matthew 5:17–20:

> Do not think that I have come to abolish the Law or the Prophets; I have not come to abolish them but to fulfill them. For truly, I say to you, until heaven and earth pass away, not an iota, not a dot, will pass from the Law until all is accomplished. Therefore whoever relaxes one of the least of these commandments and teaches others to do the same will be called least in the kingdom of heaven, but whoever does them and teaches them will be called great in the kingdom of heaven. For I tell you, unless your righteousness exceeds that of the scribes and Pharisees, you will never enter the kingdom of heaven.

The Pharisees tried to trap him into saying that it is alright to ignore some part of the law so that they could portray him as speaking against the law, but Jesus did not fall into the trap. He made it clear that God expects humanity to keep the law perfectly. He echoes the injunction in Leviticus 19:2 to "be holy, for I the LORD your God am holy" by commanding us to "be perfect, as your heavenly Father is perfect" (Matthew 5:48).

What is Jesus doing both in Matthew 5 and in Matthew 22? He is preaching the law so that we might understand how far short we fall of the perfect standard God expects of creatures made in his image. He is showing us our need of the gospel, our need of grace, our need of a Saviour. But he is also using the law to teach us what it means to live a life that is pleasing to God as Spirit-filled, New Testament believers.

So, given that Jesus uses the law of God to show us the shape of the Christian life in Matthew 5 to 7 and, given that he uses the summary of the law in Matthew 22 to reveal our need of the grace of the gospel, it seemed good to begin the catechism with Matthew 22 in order to set the stage for the gospel and conversion and then to explain the meaning of the Ten Commandments later on. This way we can do justice to both of the ways Jesus used the law.

Running through this catechism is the theme of the gospel. It breathes the spirit of evangelical theology, and the main point of evangelical theology is that everyone must be born again. To be truly evangelical is to be *evangelistic*. Christians are not *born* Christians; they must be *born again* by the Spirit of God through repentance and faith in Jesus Christ. Conversion and the Spirit-filled life are at the heart of evangelical theology because they are at the heart of the Bible and the teaching of Jesus. To the unconverted person, the law is judgement and warning. Only the born-again believer has any chance of living a life of obedience to God's will as expressed in the law and then only because of the empowering of the indwelling Holy Spirit of God.

Christianity is a religion of sin and salvation. It is not primarily a system of morality or a set of rituals for proper worship. Both morality and worship are important in the Christian life, but neither one is the means by which one *becomes* a Christian in the first place. Christianity is not a self-help program designed to help people live more successfully in this present world. It is a religion that takes sin seriously and seeks a salvation that extends into eternity. This central truth is what we need to emphasize in teaching the basics of the faith.

This is why the catechism begins with what God requires of human beings and then turns to a discussion of the gospel message in the second part that deals with the Bible and the Creed. After that foundation is in place, the crux of the catechism comes in the third part, on baptism, because this is where conversion is explained. Once we know our need (Part I) and the provision God has made to meet our need (Part II), then we are ready to consider how we actually avail ourselves of God's grace and experience new life in Christ (Part III). The rest of the catechism deals with the Christian life. We look at ethics (Part IV on the Ten Commandments), worship (Part V on the Lord's Supper), spirituality (Part VI on the Lord's Prayer) and the mission of the church (Part VII on the Great Commission).

The catechism thus begins and ends with the direct and personal commands of Jesus: the Great Commandment and the Great Commission, which remind us that the entire Christian faith is a matter of believing in, trusting and following our Lord and Saviour Jesus Christ. Now we turn to a more detailed consideration of the first question.

PART I
The Great Commandment—What God requires of us

QUESTION 1: What is the Great Commandment?

And [Jesus] said to him, "You shall love the Lord your God with all your heart and with all your soul and with all your mind. This is the great and first commandment. And a second is like it: You shall love your neighbor as yourself. On these two commandments depend all the Law and the Prophets" (Matthew 22:37–40).

It is challenging to decide how to begin the catechism. The Westminster Shorter Catechism has a justly famous opening question: "What is the chief end of man?" and the profound and memorable answer is: "Man's chief end is to glorify God and to enjoy him forever." That is a magnificent way to begin instruction in the Christian faith. The Heidelberg Catechism also has a wonderful opening question: "What is your only comfort in life and in death?" The answer is beautiful and winsome: "That I am not my own, but belong with body and soul, both in life and in death to my faithful Saviour Jesus Christ." Charles Spurgeon wisely went with the Westminster Confession opening question in his catechism. But I, however rashly, attempted a new beginning; this calls for some explanation.

Any sensible person despairs of improving on such wisdom and eloquence and I certainly do not think I have done so. But I wanted this catechism to be, not only orthodox Protestant, but also specifically *evangelical* in its substance. Therefore, I wanted to highlight the need for personal conversion on the basis of personal repentance and faith, which is the heart and soul of evangelicalism. So I wanted to focus, in this catechism, on how one becomes a Christian and that means before anything else can be said we have to deal with the fact that people are not born Christian and have to make a *personal* commitment to Jesus Christ at some point in their lives.

So section one highlights our need of salvation. That means that we start with the law before moving to the gospel. But, as I have already explained, I wanted to treat the Ten Commandments later in the catechism under the heading of Christian ethics. So, for the opening section, I went to the words the Lord Jesus Christ said in reply to a question posed by the Pharisees, who were hoping to trap him into speaking against the Law of Moses. Here is the whole passage:

> But when the Pharisees heard that he had silenced the Sadducees, they gathered together. And one of them, a lawyer, asked him a question to test him. "Teacher, which is the great commandment in the Law?" And he said to him, "You shall love the Lord your God with all your heart and with all your soul and with all your mind. This is the great and first commandment. And a second is like it: You shall love your neighbor as yourself. On these two commandments depend all the Law and the Prophets" (Matthew 22:34–40).

This little story is found between two other stories. In Matthew 22:22–33 we find the Sadducees coming to test Jesus with their question about the woman who was widowed and then married the brother of her dead husband only to be widowed again. She repeats the process, marrying all seven brothers, who all die. Then she dies and the Sadducees (who did not believe in the resurrection of the dead), asked what they thought was a "gotcha question" by asking: "In the resurrection...whose wife will she be?" Jesus tells them that they are wrong because they do not know the Scriptures or the power of God. He says that in the resurrection we will neither marry nor give in marriage but will be like the angels in that respect. He then powerfully reaffirms the doctrine of the resurrection of the dead by quoting Exodus 3:6, "I am the God of Abraham, and the God of Isaac and the God of Jacob," which proves that he is not the God of the dead but of the living. We are told that when the crowd heard this exchange they were astonished at his teaching.

Then the Pharisees, seeing that the Sadducees had struck out, thought they would give it a go and they sent a lawyer to ask the question we are considering. After Jesus handles this question with great competence, displaying a deep and intimate knowledge of the law in doing so, they are silenced as well.

At that point, in verses 41–46, Jesus decides to ask *them* a question, and it turns out to be one that reveals his messiahship and divinity. He asks the Sadducees and Pharisees whose son the Messiah is. They reply, "The son of David." Then he asks how it is then that David calls his son his Lord in Psalm 110? Jesus presses home the question of how can David call his descendent his *Lord*? The clear implication is that: (1) Jesus is the Messiah and (2) Jesus is David's Lord. Jesus is revealing his identity and claiming to be the One who the early church proclaimed him to be. We are told that no one was able to answer him and from then on no one dared to ask him any more questions.

So, Jesus is teaching with divine authority about what God expects of us. He is telling us what the entire Law of Moses, the fullest revelation of God's will for humanity up to that point in history, is all about. He is telling us the essence of what God requires of humanity.

Jesus says: "You shall love the Lord your God with all your heart and with all your soul and with all your mind. This is the great and first commandment." (Matthew 22:37–38). We are to love God, not simply cower in his presence out of fear. How are we to love him? First, we are to love him with all our *hearts*. Our love for God is not to be a matter of external bodily obedience only, but a matter of actions that spring from a heart of love. Second, we are to love him with all our *souls*. This means that we are to love him with our entire being. Our soul belongs to him and because it belongs to him will live forever. We do not fear death in the way the pagans do because for us it is not the end, but only the beginning of eternity. Third, we are to love God with all our *minds*. Faith is not anti-rational or irrational but the most perfectly rational of acts. To love God is to love the One who created us for fellowship with him. To love God is to fulfil our true nature as a human being and, therefore, to find true and perfect happiness. Nothing could be more rational than that.

But note that he says that the second commandment is like the first. Since all people bear the image of God, to love a human being is to love God in that person, and therefore, it is a form of loving God. This is why the two things—worship and ethics—are so inextricably tied together. They simply cannot be separated. To love God in our neighbour requires loving our neighbour; as Jesus says, the two commandments are very similar to each other.

When we fail to love God in the way that he ought to be loved, we fail as creatures made in his image with reason and free will. Love for God always will be demonstrated in obedience to his law. The fact that the law requires us to respect parents, refrain from murder, theft, adultery, false witness and covetousness shows that in loving God we inevitably love our neighbour.

> **QUESTION 2:** Can we keep the Great Commandment?
>
> No, we are poor, miserable sinners who constantly fail to love God perfectly as he deserves to be loved and who fail to love our neighbours as ourselves. "For all have sinned and fall short of the glory of God" (Romans 3:23).

The reality of our lives is that we often break the Ten Commandments and thus offend against both other human beings and also the God who gave the law. So Question 2 asks: "Can we keep the Great Commandment?"

If we *could* keep the Great Commandment and love both God and neighbour, as each deserves to be loved, then all would be well. We would be in communion with God and living under his blessing and in his presence. This is how it was in the Garden of Eden with our first parents, Adam and Eve, before the great disaster. But now it is different, as the answer to this question makes clear. The catechism introduces the doctrine of original sin at this point. We live in a fallen state, cut off from the original innocence of the Garden, and we know ourselves, if we are honest, as miserable sinners who constantly fail to obey the Great Commandment.

All have sinned. This is the clear and unequivocal message given by the entire Bible from Genesis 3 onward. We have quoted just one verse that explicitly states that sin is universal, but we could have quoted dozens, even hundreds, of verses that affirm the reality of sin as a universal human condition at this stage of human history. The whole Bible is the record of humanity under sin being redeemed by God's actions in Jesus Christ.

It is crucial that the convert, the new Christian, the one seeking instruction in the Christian faith, come to grips with the doctrine of original sin and the consequent guilt under which we live as poor, lost, miserable, hopeless sinners:

> For the wages of sin is death, but the free gift of God is eternal life in Christ Jesus our Lord (Romans 6:23).

In Genesis 3 the mystery of why we human beings are unable to love God and our neighbour as we ought to do is explained. Adam and Eve were placed in a perfect Garden and given everything they needed. But God wanted them to have the choice to love him; he did not want them to be robots or animals, which have no free will. As rational creatures made in his image with free will, they were capable of loving God freely.

So in order to give them an opportunity to obey freely as a demonstration of their love for God, they were given a command not to eat of the tree of the knowledge of good and evil (Genesis 2:16–17). They were to let God determine what is good and what is evil rather than taking into their own hands the authority to determine what is good and what is evil. Would they love God as God and recognize that as Creator it was his right to say what is right for them as creatures and what is wrong? The eating of the fruit was symbolic of an entire attitude of life in which they were either going to rely on God's Word as the authority for their lives or they were going to try and play God themselves and decide for themselves what is good and what is evil. Is ethics going to be based on the divine command or on the human will? This was the choice, and they made the wrong one.

They ate the forbidden fruit and claimed the prerogative of God to determine what is good and what is evil. And this is what their descendants have been doing ever since. Humans claim to be able to decide what should be called evil and what should be called good and to change God's laws to suit themselves. The problem is this leads humans to try to fight reality, since God's laws are consistent with God's creation. So when we try to change those laws, we find ourselves at odds with reality. This leads to grief in every situation. The history of the world is the history of the disaster that followed from this evil choice.

The real problem is not just that we break God's laws from time to time. If this were the problem, then it would be true that some of us would hardly sin at all for long stretches of time. In that case, we could convince ourselves that we barely need God's forgiveness and that we are good enough as we are. But the real problem is that we *are* sinners, that is, we have a fallen, sinful nature that makes it impossible for us to do the right thing in every case. We are guilty both for what we have *done*—which is bad enough—but we are also guilty for what we *are*. We are under God's judgement and facing God's wrath because we are sinners.

This insight makes it clear how hopeless our situation is. We don't have to turn over a new leaf or make a New Year's resolution to be good. We can't just decide not to sin anymore and expect that God will be impressed with our righteousness. No, the problem is that we are sinners by nature and without God and without hope. We are sinners by virtue of having a fallen, sinful nature inherited from our first parents: Adam and Eve. We deserve to die because of who we are: lost, sinful, compromised, weak and miserable sinners.

So we need a Saviour, not just an example. We need transformation, not just forgiveness. We need to become new people, not just to start acting more obediently. We need forgiveness but we need more than forgiveness. Our problem is not that we are sick and need to get better, but that, as Paul puts it in Ephesians 2:1–6, we are dead and need resurrection!

Only when all this becomes crystal clear to us and we stop fighting God's assessment of our condition and agree with God that we are poor, miserable, lost sinners without any hope of our own are we are ready really to hear the gospel. Once we do hear the gospel, the depths of our depravity and the degree of our degradation and lostness becomes increasingly clear.

QUESTION 3: Is there any hope for us?

Yes, but only if we believe in Jesus Christ as our only hope of salvation.

Paradoxically, the degree to which there is or is not hope for a person is the very degree to which that person accepts the grim and foreboding message of the answer to Question 2. The more clearly we see our need, the more clearly we see that we need the gospel. The person who does not really understand how lost he is cannot see why the radical message of the gospel can possibly be true. Why would the Son of God have to die on the cross in order to help basically good people find the right road? Good question. He wouldn't have had to die if we are basically good people who just need a little guidance and help along the way. The person who does not really understand the gospel also labours under the delusion that it is possible to save oneself by human effort to do good works.

If we think salvation is something we can accomplish ourselves—perhaps with a little assistance from God along the way—then we will never trust Christ for salvation. Therefore, the answer to Question 3 is, "Yes, but only if we believe in Jesus Christ as our only hope of salvation." Are you desperate enough to realize that you only have one hope and that is Jesus Christ? Are you truly convinced that on your own you have only judgement, wrath and hell to look forward to? Are you really sure that you cannot put your trust in yourself, or in religion, or in ethics or in anything else in all creation?

Yes, there is hope for us poor, miserable sinners. But our hope is not in our own righteousness, which the Bible calls "filthy rags" (Isaiah 64:6 KJV). Our hope is in him who lived for us, died for us and rose for us. He did for us what we could never have done for ourselves, and it is for this reason that he is our Saviour.

Questions for reflection

1. Have you ever heard the gospel presented as a solution to practical problems of living in this world, rather than as salvation from sin?

2. What are the three purposes of the law? Can you give an example of how God has used the law to shape your understanding of what it means to live a holy life?

3. What does the author mean by saying: "We are guilty both for what we have *done*...but we are also guilty for what we *are?*"

4. In the Genesis 3 story of the Fall into sin, how did the serpent bring Eve to the point of disobedience? Describe the process as recounted in the text. What insights into the nature of temptation can we draw from this narrative?

5. What are the two commands of Jesus with which the catechism begins and ends? Have you committed them both to memory?

3

If the Bible is God's Word, why do we need creeds?

PART II
The Bible and the Apostles' Creed—Christian doctrine
QUESTIONS 4–8

> "Some people say the Bible is all we need,
> but the creed helps keep us biblical."

INTRODUCTION

There are only two approaches to authority in religious and moral matters: either each individual constitutes an authority for himself or else we accept an external authority over us. It cannot be both simultaneously. Either I am the final authority or something else is. Individualism is not unique to our highly individualistic modern society; it is as old as the human race. Eve was tempted by Satan to want to be "like God knowing good and evil" (Genesis 3:5). God was Eve's authority, and it was God who determined whether or not it was permissible to eat of the fruit of the tree of the knowledge of good and evil. But Satan convinced her to usurp God's place (as Satan himself had done) and set herself up as an authority for herself. This is the essence of individualism. We decide what is good and what is evil, what is true and what is false, what is beneficial and what is harmful for ourselves. Individualism, therefore, is closely related to original sin.

Sometimes we hear people say, "We need no creed but the Bible," and it sounds like a ringing endorsement of biblical authority. It sounds pious and right; it sounds like the person is bowing to no authority but God alone. It sounds like the person is placing himself humbly under the authority of Scripture. But it may not be as simple as that; individualism is very insidious and takes many forms. It actually turns out that a sneaky kind of individualism can lurk behind this seemingly humble claim because it turns out that many of those who say this really mean that *they* will interpret what the Bible says for themselves without acknowledging the tradition of the church, the wisdom of the elders or the guidance of the Holy Spirit over the past 2,000 years. Many of those who started cults or heretical offshoots of Christianity had the very same slogan: "No creed but the Bible"—meaning, of course, "No creed but the Bible *as interpreted by me*." This slogan can be a club with which one bashes tradition and orthodoxy and sets oneself up as the ultimate authority in the church.

Of course, we acknowledge with the Protestant Reformers the full authority of the Scripture over the church. Scripture is a higher authority than human reason, than church tradition or our own experience. Scripture is also a higher authority than any extra-biblical creed, and the best of the orthodox creeds that have stood the test of time are actually short summaries of the meaning of Scripture itself. Creeds arise from careful study of the Bible and its message, and their function is to guard and preserve the true interpretation of Scripture. The Bible is in a class all by itself because it alone is inspired by the Holy Spirit and without error. But the Reformers would have been horrified by the attitude that we could or should try to read and interpret the Bible all by ourselves without help and guidance from the saints, bishops, doctors and teachers of the past centuries. They did not do that in their own writings; they sought to be learners in the church and to benefit from the wisdom of teachers from every century.

Having a high view of the authority of Scripture is a necessary but not sufficient condition for having a sound, orthodox theology. In fact, heretical groups like the Jehovah's Witnesses believe in the full inspiration and authority of Scripture and yet are still heretics. What we really need to do is to believe in the true and historically orthodox *interpretation* of Scripture, and that is where the creeds come in. The Protestant Reformers sought to reform the church by the standards of Scripture, but they saw the creeds of the first five centuries such as the Apostles' Creed, the Nicene Creed and the Definition of Chalcedon as true summaries of biblical teaching and as aids to them in their task of weeding out more recent heretical teachings that had crept into the medieval church. The creeds are not an alternative to a high view of Scriptural authority, but rather are aids to sound doctrine. In this chapter, we will examine how this works out in practice.

DEFINING THE CHRISTIAN FAITH

In Part I of the catechism, we saw that all human beings are called to a life of perfect love in imitation of God our heavenly Father, and that we are to love God with all our hearts, all our souls and all our minds. And we are to love our neighbour as ourselves. Jesus says that these two commandments sum up and include all the law and the Prophets. Far from taking away from the law or watering down its radical demands or subtracting the harder commandments from the law, Jesus intensifies the demand of the law to the point where we realize we cannot possibly hope to live the life God demands we live. Thus we realize how true the Bible is in saying that "all have sinned and fall short of the glory of God" (Romans 2:23).

If this were all we ever heard of God's Word, this realization of our helplessness to save ourselves and our hopelessness in the face of impending judgement, it could drive us to despair and suicide. But if we stammer out the hesitant and plaintive question, "Is there any hope for us?" we suddenly hear a note of grace burst through the gloom, lighting up our hearts and infusing us with hope, "Yes, but only if we believe in Jesus Christ as our only hope of salvation."

Upon hearing this ray of hope, we are utterly transfixed by the one possible way of escape from the impending judgement. If we really understand the seriousness of our situation and the slim ray of hope that filters through the clouds of divine wrath, we cannot take our eyes off of that ray of light. We cannot think of anything but that glorious, divine, beautiful name—the name of Jesus Christ.

Where can we learn more about him? What does it mean to believe in him? Who is he? What does he teach? How can I find him? These are the questions that we cannot stop asking.

PART II
The Bible and the Apostles' Creed—Christian doctrine

In Part II of the catechism, we consider what it means to believe in Jesus Christ. One cannot be saved by believing just *any* set of teachings one wants to believe, and there are conflicting doctrines regarding Jesus Christ. Since our salvation depends on knowing and trusting the true Jesus Christ, we need to know the *truth* about Jesus Christ.

So we turn our attention to the five questions that focus our study today:

1. What does it mean to believe in Jesus Christ?
2. What is the Bible?
3. What is the message of the Bible?

4. Is there a convenient and reliable way to sum up the biblical message?

5. What does the Apostles' Creed say?

QUESTION 4: What does it mean to believe in Jesus Christ?

It means to believe the message of the Bible because the Bible reveals Jesus Christ.

Why are evangelical Christians so fixated on studying the Bible? The explanation is given in the answer to this question of what it means to believe in Jesus Christ: "It means to believe the message of the Bible because the Bible reveals Jesus Christ." We study the Bible so diligently because we believe that the Bible reveals Jesus Christ. Many people have only a very vague idea of who Jesus Christ is and what it means to believe in him. This is not a new phenomenon. During his earthly ministry, as we read in the Gospels, there was a wide range of opinion on who Jesus was.

One day, as Mark 8 records, Jesus asked his disciples who the people were saying he was. They replied that some thought he was John the Baptist risen from the dead, some thought he was Elijah, while others thought he was one of the prophets. People might have thought he was Elijah because Malachi 3:1 predicts that a "messenger of the covenant" (often thought to be Elijah) would return prior to the coming of Day of the Lord. But according to Jesus, "Elijah" had already come in the person of John the Baptist (Matthew 17:12).

This means that Jesus was not merely a preacher of repentance preparing Israel for the reception of a still future Messiah. That was what John the Baptist was. He was given the task of preparing Israel to receive her Messiah in the person of Jesus Christ by calling people to repent and live in expectation of the imminent coming of the Messiah. He preached sin and the need to repent. But John's baptism was not Spirit baptism. John had no message of forgiveness of sin except insofar as he pointed forward to the coming Messiah. In this respect, John was the last of the Old Testament prophets.

Jesus was not John the Baptist, but rather the one who comes after John, the one to whom John pointed when he said, "Behold, the Lamb of God, who takes away the sin of the world!" (John 1:29). Jesus was not merely a preacher of repentance and preparation—he was the Saviour of the world who fulfilled the Old Testament prophecies and actually accomplished salvation on the cross.

It also means that Jesus is not merely the human forerunner of a greater one. Many people believe this today. They see Jesus as a great figure, but not the *final* revelation for all time. For example, this is what Islam teaches: Jesus is a great prophet but Mohammed is greater. Mormons think Jesus' mission had to be completed by Joseph Smith and the further revelations he received. The Unification Church thinks that its founder is the final revelation and Jesus was just a forerunner. But Jesus is the final and full revelation of God as Hebrews 1 so clearly teaches.

Jesus is also not merely one of the prophets. Many people today have been deceived into believing this by false teachers known as liberal Protestants. They see Jesus as a good moral teacher and an inspiring example, but in the end, just a great man and not God in the flesh. For them, Jesus is one of the many prophets in Scripture and, while he may be regarded as the greatest one of them all, he is finally just a human being like them. People made this mistake during Jesus's lifetime on earth, after his death and down through the centuries.

How do we make sure that we know the real Jesus Christ? When there is so much false information floating around and there are so many divergent opinions about who Jesus really is, how can we be sure that we know the real Jesus?

The obvious answer is that we need to know the teaching of Jesus Christ himself. But how do we do that? In the Great Commission, Jesus commands his disciples to teach all new converts all that he has commanded:

> Go therefore and make disciples of all nations, baptizing them in the name of the Father and of the Son and of the Holy Spirit, teaching them to observe all that I have commanded you. And behold, I am with you always, to the end of the age (Matthew 28:19–20).

Jesus is very explicit about what new converts to the faith are to be taught: "all that I have commanded you." But how do we determine exactly what Jesus has commanded us? We do not have him living among us in the flesh like the apostles did. We do not have the chance to hear him speak and ask him questions like they did. We do not have direct access to his words, teachings, doctrines and so on, except through one avenue: The Bible.

To make the Bible our sole authority for knowing what to believe about Jesus Christ is to let the biblical revelation itself shape our beliefs and convictions. We can put our trust in the Jesus Christ of the Bible. But this leads naturally to our next question: What is the Bible?

QUESTION 5: What is the Bible?

It is the inerrant and infallible Word of God written for our instruction. As Paul teaches Timothy, "All Scripture is breathed out by God and profitable for teaching, for reproof, for correction, and for training in righteousness, that the man of God may be complete, equipped for every good work" (2 Timothy 3:16–17).

In this answer, we learn two basic things about the nature of Scripture: It is *inerrant* and it is *infallible*. To say that the Bible is inerrant is to say that it is true in all that God teaches through the Bible. It is to say that the Bible leads us into truth and never leads us astray. The Bible is inspired, which means that it was "breathed out by God." The Bible is not merely the work of human authors, it also has a divine author who speaks through the human authors and gives it a unified message. If the Bible appears to teach something that is clearly not true, it must mean that either there is something wrong with our interpretation or that we are mistaken and what it teaches actually is true.

Some people like to zero in on minor issues in the Bible and attempt to find some picky, little error so that they can say that the Bible is not inerrant. It is very important to some people to be able to do this because they want to evade or negate some biblical teaching that is inconvenient for their lives. They want to undermine biblical authority, and they think it can be done if they just look for a little error somewhere in the Bible.

But we have to remember that God gave the Bible through human beings who wrote at particular times on the basis of the customs and conventions of their day, and he did not bother to correct them or cause them to write according to the conventions of our day just so we would not be offended. For example, in the matter of quotations of the Old Testament, we do not see the kind of exact, word-for-word quotations we expect to see in books today. The ideal of a perfect, word-for-word quotation of an Old Testament text is something that only became expected after the invention of the printing press in the sixteenth century. This invention caused the rise of the attitude that a valid quotation *must* be word-for-word perfect. Ancient authors frequently quoted from memory and did not place a high premium on the exact wording, although they cared very much about getting the *sense* of the quotation right. What they valued was the exact and true *meaning*. So many New Testament quotations of Old Testament texts are not letter perfect and that is not considered an error.

To take another example, because we do not have the original manuscripts of the biblical books, but only copies, we often are uncertain about the exact reading of a given verse. Sometimes the existing families of manuscripts do not agree. But no such disagreement affects any major doctrine, and no doctrine rests on a disputed reading alone.

When we speak of the Bible as inerrant, we are not applying modern standards of writing to ancient documents. Rather, we are speaking of the truth of the message, and we are affirming that we hold ourselves obligated to believe whatever Scripture teaches. We do not contradict Scripture, we do not go beyond Scripture, and we do not neglect Scripture. Instead we affirm it, we study it and we let it function in our lives as our authority, because in Scripture we hear God speaking directly and authoritatively to us.

We also believe that the Bible is infallible; by this we mean that the things Paul speaks of it being useful for in 2 Timothy 3:16–17 are done by Scripture without error. This is to say, Scripture is infallible when used for teaching, for reproof, for correction and for training in righteousness. When we use it for what it was designed and given by God for, then we will see that it never fails to make us competent and equipped for every good work. The Bible is sufficient and clear when we read it with open hearts, as well as open minds. The Bible is the inerrant and infallible Word of God, and it is the basis for our faith.

QUESTION 6: What is the message of the Bible?

The message of the Bible is that Jesus Christ is the Son of God, the Son of Man and the Lord and Saviour of the world. The Old Testament consists of the writings of the prophets who foretold the coming of Jesus Christ, and the New Testament consists of the writings of the apostles who explain prophecies.

The answer to this question stresses the centrality of Jesus Christ in the Bible. The Bible consists of two Testaments, the Old and the New, and they both have Jesus Christ at their centre. Therefore, they constitute the church's one Bible—a unified book with a unified message. What is that message?

The biblical message about Jesus Christ has four main parts: that he is (1) the Son of God, (2) the Son of Man, (3) the Lord, and (4) the Saviour of the world. We will consider each one in turn.

1. Jesus Christ is the Son of God.

The phrase "Son of God" has wide and various usages in Scripture. It can be used for the Davidic kings, and it can be used of angels. But its main use in the New Testament is as a Christological title that points to the divinity of Jesus Christ. As the identity of Jesus Christ is gradually unfolded in the Bible, we come to see clearly that when he is called "Son of God" the meaning goes deeper than it does with any other person. It points to his unity of being with the Father, that is, to his essential deity. He is the Son of God, the real thing to which all the others merely point as types of him.

2. Jesus Christ is the Son of Man.

The title of "Son of Man" has a dual meaning. In the Gospels, it was used by Jesus of himself, and here it means "human being" or "man" as it does throughout the book of Ezekiel. It has a rather general meaning that is not specifically referring to his divine identity. The meaning of this title in Daniel 7:13–14 is quite different. There it refers to the heavenly Son of Man who appears on the clouds of heaven and is given a kingdom as an everlasting dominion that does not pass away. Jesus claims this title in its Danielic sense at his trial before the Sanhedrin (Mark 14:62). Both meanings apply to Jesus.

Throughout the Scriptures we find teaching about both the divinity and the humanity of Jesus Christ. Each passage must be interpreted carefully in reference to one or the other, and they must not be confused. The Bible teaches that Jesus Christ is both the eternally begotten Word of the Father and the incarnate Word that has assumed a human nature to himself.

3. Jesus Christ is the Lord.

The title "Lord" indicates not only the fact that Jesus Christ is destined to rule over all creation, but also his divinity. In the Greek version of the Hebrew Old Testament, which was used by the New Testament writers, it is significant that the Greek word *kurios* (translated as "Lord" in English) was used by the translators to translate the Hebrew *Yahweh* into Greek. So when the New Testament writers call Jesus "Lord," which they very frequently do, they are applying to him the same word that is used to translate the Old Testament name for the God of Israel. Thus, we can see that it is an ascription of deity to call Jesus "Lord."

4. Jesus Christ is the Saviour of the world.

This final phrase, "Saviour of the world," captures the essence of the biblical message about who Jesus is in a single phrase. To call Jesus Christ the Saviour is to presuppose the problem of sin and the reality of the wrath of God from which he saves us. It is also to imply that he is divine, because he does for us not only what we could never have done for ourselves but also that which only God could do.

The predictions of the Messiah by the prophets of the Old Testament and the witness to Christ's coming in fulfilment of those prophecies by the apostles of the New Testament give unity to the Bible. Together the Old Testament and the New Testament make up a complete witness to Jesus Christ.

This is why the Old Testament ends with a note of expectation, anticipation and unfulfilled promise. God began his work of redemption in the history of Israel, but as the Old Testament draws to a close, it is clear that full redemption has not yet come. Malachi 3 speaks of the coming "Day of the Lord," which is a prophecy of the day of judgement at Christ's second coming, and it also speaks of how God would send Elijah to preach repentance and turn the hearts of the people toward God in preparation for that day of purification and judgement. The Old Testament prophets saw glimpses of both the first and second comings of Christ, and they puzzled, as Peter testifies in 1 Peter 1:10–12, over what it all meant and how all would be fulfilled.

The New Testament, on the other hand, ends in a completely different way. In the final chapter of the Bible, we read a warning not to add to or take away anything from this book (Revelation 22:18–19). Why does it say that? It is stressing the completion of divine revelation. Once Jesus Christ has come, we have seen the definitive revelation of God for all time. This is why the next thing on the agenda of world history is the *second* coming of Christ.

We have in the Bible a complete and adequate witness to Jesus Christ. When he commands us to teach "all that I have commanded you," we obey by teaching the Bible. This is why the Bible is the text for every sermon every week and the subject of our study in various other settings during the week. The Bible is the textbook, and the church is the school of discipleship.

QUESTION 7: Is there a convenient and reliable way to sum up the biblical message?

Yes, the Apostles' Creed is a short summary of the biblical message that has been used in the church since the second century.

QUESTION 8: What does the Apostles' Creed say?

I believe in God, the Father almighty,
creator of heaven and earth.

I believe in Jesus Christ, God's only Son, our Lord,
who was conceived by the Holy Spirit,
born of the Virgin Mary,

suffered under Pontius Pilate,
was crucified, died, and was buried;
he descended to the dead.
On the third day he rose again;
he ascended into heaven,
he is seated at the right hand of the Father,
and he will come again to judge the living and the dead.

I believe in the Holy Spirit,
the holy catholic church,
the communion of saints,
the forgiveness of sins,
the resurrection of the body
and the life everlasting. Amen.

For as long as the Bible has existed, there has been a need to ensure that it is interpreted correctly. After all, the Bible consists of sixty-six books, written by over forty different authors, in three different languages, over a period of over 1,500 years. It is a long, complex and challenging book to read and interpret. Yet, there is a unity and coherence because of the inspiration of the Holy Spirit.

The church has always believed that we humans can understand the Bible precisely because God has given it to us for the purpose of teaching us what we need to know about Jesus Christ. As we interpret individual verses or passages, we need to keep in mind the overall message of the Bible. This creed was an attempt to articulate the overall message of the Bible in a short format that could easily be memorized and kept at the forefront of one's mind as one reads the Bible.

The Apostles' Creed is not meant to be a higher authority than Scripture; rather, it is derived from Scripture. We all believe in a certain interpretation of Scripture; no one has direct and unmediated access into the mind of God such that we have no need to interpret the text that we are reading. When we use the Apostles' Creed to help guide our interpretation, we are allowing the traditional, orthodox tradition of the Church to guide us in our interpretation. Not to do this would be to imply that the church has always been wrong and we alone have direct access to the truth, and that would be the same kind of pride that led Satan to rebel against God in the first place. To let the Apostles' Creed guide our interpretation is not to exalt a human document above the Bible; it is an act of humility that shows that we recognize that we all need teachers and that we all can benefit from the wisdom of past centuries of faithful Christians.

CONCLUSION

In order to know what it means to believe in Jesus Christ we must know the Bible, and one key way to be sure we have understood the Bible and interpreted it correctly is to study the Apostles' Creed and let it be our guide to sound biblical interpretation. When we interpret the Bible in harmony with the Apostles' Creed, we are sure to interpret it in such a way that the centrality of Jesus Christ emerges clearly into view.

Questions for reflection

1. Have you ever observed a person who set out to interpret the Bible alone, with no help from anyone else, go astray in the process? What did that person end up teaching?

2. What four titles of Jesus Christ sum up the message of the Bible? State briefly what each title means.

3. Why is it the case that the Apostles' Creed is not a higher authority than the Bible?

4

What is the significance of the structure of the Apostles' Creed?

PART II
The Bible and the Apostles' Creed—Christian doctrine
QUESTIONS 9–11

"The shape of the Apostles' Creed reflects
the shape of the triune God."

INTRODUCTION

A.W. Tozer once wrote: "What comes into our minds when we think about God is the most important thing about us."[1] He was right. What a person believes about God is more important than his or her racial identity, place of birth, nationality, level of education, marital status, financial means, personality type or any other characteristic by which people define themselves. The Bible agrees with Tozer as well, for we read in Deuteronomy:

Take care lest your heart be deceived, and you turn aside and serve other gods and worship them; then the anger of the LORD will be kindled against you, and he will shut up the heavens, so that there will be

---

[1] A.W. Tozer, *The Knowledge of the Holy* (New York: Harper One, 1961), 1.

no rain, and the land will yield no fruit, and you will perish quickly off the good land that the LORD is giving you (Deuteronomy 11:16–17).

As the children of Israel were preparing to finally enter Canaan after forty years of useless wandering in the wilderness, Moses warns them against being seduced by other gods. The land of Canaan was full of the grossest and most vile sorts of idolatry, and God knew that the children of Israel would be tempted to join the crowd, get in step, go with the flow and do the fashionable thing—if not because they actually wanted to do so, then perhaps because they wanted to blend in with the world and not stick out as fanatics, holier-than-thou types who showed their superiority by clinging to the worship of one God only.

It is easy to see evangelical Christians today are in a similarly dangerous situation as the ancient Israelites. As my wife and I drive home from church on Sunday morning, we drive past a mosque, and the traffic from a nearby Hindu temple sometimes holds us up. A Jehovah's Witness building is located just a block away from our house. Where we live in the Greater Toronto Area we have cults, new religions, world religions and every type of idolatry all around us.

We live in a society characterized by great religious diversity, just like the early church. But the outright worship of literal, physical idols is not a great temptation for many of us. We have more beguiling temptations. For example, we live in a materialistic culture that makes idols out of sex, money and a hedonistic lifestyle. We are often tempted to reconstruct God in our own image. Many people claim to be worshipping the one true God but, in reality, are worshipping a creation of their own imagination with the label of the biblical God slapped on it.

The questions are: Which God do you serve? Do you serve the triune God revealed in the Bible? Do you know what the God of biblical revelation is actually like? Or do you have your own "imagined god" that you call the God of the Bible? The goal of this chapter is to provide the biblical tools and the theological understanding to answer these questions accurately.

QUESTION 9: What does it mean to believe in the Creed?

It means to hold resolutely to the truth of these statements, which are a summary of the contents of the Holy Scriptures and the sole basis of my hope of eternal salvation.

We need to understand that the Creed contains a *summary* of the gospel, which identifies the true God of the Bible. The God of Scripture is the only true God, the One who created the world and who is redeeming it through his Holy Spirit on the basis of the work of Jesus Christ—this is what we must believe in order to be saved, to be real Christians and not just "Christians in name only." Salvation is not possible apart from believing in the true God.

I. THE STRUCTURE OF THE APOSTLES' CREED

The answer to Question 10 explains the key to grasping the structure of the Apostles' Creed.

QUESTION 10: Why is the Creed given in three articles?

Each article corresponds to one of the three persons of the Holy Trinity: God the Father, God the Son and God the Holy Spirit.

1. Its Trinitarian structure

As you read the Apostles' Creed you will note that it divides naturally into what are called the three articles. Each article focuses on one person of the Holy Trinity: Father, Son and Holy Spirit. Each article also focuses on the work of the triune God: creation, reconciliation and redemption.

The Father created the world through the Son and Spirit and rules providentially over it. The Son is the one sent by the Father who accomplishes the salvation of the world through his death, resurrection, ascension and second coming. The Father and Son send the Holy Spirit, whose works include the forgiveness of sins, the creation of the church, the resurrection of the body and the granting of life everlasting. The doctrine of the Trinity is presupposed and implicit within the very structure of the Creed.

2. Its narrative structure

We also should note that the Creed tells a story. This story begins with the Old Testament and the creation of the world in the first article. It continues with a brief summary of the life of Jesus in the second article, and it concludes with events, which are either currently in process (the church, forgiveness of sins) or future (resurrection of the body, life everlasting) in the third article. These latter events bring the history of creation to its conclusion.

The Creed thus serves as a brief overview of Scripture and instructs the church in the present era to confess the source of its faith in the Old Testament God of Israel and the continuity between the Creator God and

Jesus Christ. We shouldn't be tempted to think that the Creed is an adequate replacement for Scripture—that is not its purpose. Rather, the Creed is meant to be a guide to reading Scripture. While reading any particular verse or passage in the Bible, one should always keep in mind the big picture, the overall plot, the main message.

You will further notice that the article dealing with the Son of God, Jesus Christ, is the longest of the three articles and is placed in the centre of the other two. This reflects the fact that Jesus Christ is absolutely central to the Bible. The narrative of his pre-existence, birth, ministry, death, resurrection, ascension and return as judge is the centre of biblical revelation. All of Scripture—including poetry and prayers, law and gospel, wisdom and epistles, history and prophecy—should be read and interpreted in the light of Jesus Christ.

One more thing to notice is that the second article has active verbs, which the first and third articles lack. They consist mainly of lists, whereas the second article is a series of actions expressed via verbs: born, crucified, died, buried, descended, rose, ascended, seated, come and judge. This is another way we can see the centrality of the second article. The first and third articles frame this central narrative.

This narrative is the overarching story Christians believe is the true and comprehensive story of the universe. Every other story must be fit into this one, including the story of our lives, the story of our nation, church history and so on. The criteria by which we can judge whether or not our lives are meaningful is whether or not, and to the extent that, the story of our lives fits well into this master story. This is how Christians find meaning in life; everything from the fall of the Roman empire to my grandmother getting cancer to the mystery of why human beings are so often tempted by sexual sin—every part of human experience has to fit somewhere in the overall narrative structure of the Christian faith. We attempt to make sense of the small and local stories of our lives in the context of the comprehensive, overarching, biblical story, which centres on Jesus Christ.

Note that the story we live in and our conception of God are intricately interrelated. In pantheism, the blind, meaningless forces of nature become objects of worship. In atheistic Marxism, man is called to take control of history and usher in the classless society by fomenting revolution. Man replaces divine providence, because if there is no God, someone has to take charge. Marxism explains the existence of the world as a matter of blind chance and calls human beings to take charge of making sure that history turns out right. This means, ultimately, man becomes God. Other modern versions of the "man becomes God" type of religion include Progressivism and Darwinism. In all three of these so-called "secular religions," we see an attempt to create a giant framework or story into which all aspects of life can be fit. The biblical narrative, as summarized in the Apostles' Creed, is an alternative to these false narratives, and the biblical God is an alternative to human self-worship or nature-worship. Human beings are made in such a way that we always end up worshipping something. If we do not worship the true God of Scripture, then we worship either ourselves, idols or nature. These options exhaust the possible alternatives.

II. THE CREED AND THE DOCTRINE OF THE TRINITY

What is the implication of saying "I believe" in God the Father, Jesus Christ and the Holy Spirit? Why does the Creed make these three statements?

1. We believe in God, not in doctrines about God.
First, note that we are not instructed to believe in the authority of Scripture or the virgin birth or the resurrection of Jesus. We are instructed to believe in God the Father, God the Son and God the Holy Spirit. We believe in the triune God, not the doctrine of the Trinity. Why point this out?

What I am trying to show is that the Creed points us in the direction of a *personal* relationship with a *personal* God. The Christian God has a name: God the Father, Son and Holy Spirit, the triune One. God is personal; God is not an abstract idea or a doctrine or a proposition. God is a personal being in whom we can believe or not believe, love or not love, serve or not serve, worship or not worship, follow or not follow, listen to or not listen to.

I hope that anyone who thinks that the Creed is a relic of ritualism, exhibit "A" of formalistic religion, a bit of religious mumbo jumbo for non-born-again churchgoers, will set those wrong ideas aside. Of course, the Creed can be highjacked in the service of formal religiosity and has been in the history of the church—as have the sermon, the Lord's Prayer, the Ten Commandments, the catechism, practices like kneeling, crossing oneself, taking communion, baptism, meditation, singing hymns, reciting psalms and a hundred other things. My point is that we don't just jettison all these things automatically. We can't simply decide to practice Christianity without doing anything that was done by Christians who lived prior to the Reformation, or the seventeenth century or whenever our denomination started—although I must say that Baptists, Brethren and some contemporary community churches sometimes give it a good try.

The Creed asks us, actually requires us, to believe *directly* in God. You cannot recite the Creed with integrity if you don't have a personal relationship with the triune God revealed to us in the Holy Scriptures.

2. Doctrines keep us from error in interpreting the Bible.
If we believe directly in God, and not in doctrines, then why is the Creed

full of doctrines? It is simple really. Doctrines help us believe in the true God. Doctrines are like rules or guidelines that prevent us from going off the rails as we read, interpret and teach one another the Bible. The main doctrine of Christianity is the doctrine of the Trinity. This doctrine tells us who God is and helps us focus on whom we are talking about when we say the word "God."

III. THE MEANING OF THE DOCTRINE OF THE TRINITY

QUESTION 11: What does it mean to say that God is the Holy Trinity?

It means that God is three persons and one being, and therefore, he is one God. In his essence, God is beyond our human understanding, but we can be sure that we know him truly because he has revealed himself in history to Israel, in Holy Scripture and supremely and finally in Jesus Christ.

1. The doctrine of the Trinity says that God is one being in three persons.

The doctrine of the Trinity says that God is one being and three persons. God is three persons sharing one common being. One being, three persons; that is the essence of the doctrine of the Trinity. But what are we getting at here? What does this mean?

Unfortunately, all the illustrations of the Trinity from nature and from human nature—such as the clover (three petals and one plant), water (as ice, vapour and liquid), the human person (as mind, body and soul)—are all inadequate. The petals on a clover are each part of the plant, but they are each only *part* of the plant. God the Father is fully God, God the Son is fully God and God the Holy Spirit is fully God. The water molecules are not *simultaneously* ice, water and vapour. They just change from one state into the other. But God is Father, Son and Holy Spirit continuously. A human being is a person but parts of a human being such as mind or soul are not persons in their own right. Nothing from the created order can really function as an illustration of the Trinity, because God is the infinite Creator of all and totally beyond any such comparison. God is unique.

I also need to warn you that there is a real translation problem with the term "person" for us who live in the modern world. The modern concept of a person is quite different from what the fourth-century church fathers meant when they used the Greek word that gets translated "person" in formulating the doctrine of the Trinity. When those church fathers used the word *hypostasis* (Greek) or *persona* (Latin), which are translated in

English by "person," these terms did not have the individualistic connotations that the modern English word "person" has today. We think of a person as an autonomous being, a self-contained centre of consciousness. We have human rights, which are defined individualistically. We view the person as prior to all relationships, including even family relationships. We see each individual as an independent centre of meaning who is free to enter into and withdraw from relationships as the sovereign determiner of his or her own fate. So, as a society, we have easy divorce, abortion on demand and slogans like, "be true to yourself," "the right of self-determination" and "be your own person."

Now it should be obvious what the problem is in referring to God the Father, God the Son and God the Holy Spirit as "persons." They are not presented in Scripture as persons in the modern sense at all. In the Gospel of John, Jesus says:

For I have come down from heaven, not to do my own will but the will of him who sent me. (John 6:38).

I and the Father are one (John 10:30).

These things I have spoken to you while I am still with you. But the Helper, the Holy Spirit, whom the Father will send in my name, he will teach you all things and bring to your remembrance all that I have said to you (John 14:25–26).

But when the Helper comes, whom I will send to you from the Father, the Spirit of truth, who proceeds from the Father, he will bear witness about me (John 15:26).

When the Spirit of truth comes, he will guide you into all the truth, for he will not speak on his own authority, but whatever he hears he will speak, and he will declare to you the things that are to come. He will glorify me, for he will take what is mine and declare it to you. All that the Father has is mine; therefore I said that he will take what is mine and declare it to you (John 16:13–15).

These sayings show that although the three persons of the Trinity are distinguishable, they are not *autonomous* or *independent* in the modern sense of the word "person" at all.

This translation problem has led some theologians to substitute the phrase "mode of being" for the word "person," as in "one God in three modes of being." But the problem is that "mode of being" does not convey the personal nature of God as well as the word "person." So there is no perfect terminology. We are struggling with the limitations of language in describing what is beyond the capacity of human language to contain. We just have to let Scripture redefine what "person" means when it is applied to God. (Our modern concept of the human person is theologically dreadful and should be redefined as well, but that is a matter for another time.)

The statement that God is one being or one essence means that all three persons are *equally* and *fully* God. They all are of the same essential nature; they are actually the same essence not merely three examples of a certain kind of essence the way that Peter, James and John all have essences that belong to the category "human." Peter, James and John are three separate human beings and their natures or essences are similar but not the same. In God, the Father, Son and Spirit are not three members of the class of things with a divine essence. They are *one* essence.

The only distinction between them is that the Son is begotten by the Father and the Spirit proceeds from the Father and the Son. So they differ only in their relationships to one another. The Father is not the Son or the Spirit, the Son is not the Father or the Spirit and the Spirit is not the Father or the Son. Apart from being *distinguishable* in their relationships to one another, *they are one in every other way*. They are one in value, one in substance, one in power and authority, and one in being. They have one will and one mind and one purpose. The doctrine of the inseparability of operations says that when one member of the Trinity is at work, all three are actually working together. They could never be at odds with each other or opposed to each other or willing conflicting objectives.

2. The doctrine of the Trinity is the only way to make sense of Scripture.

This doctrine is not easy to understand. It is challenging even to think about. The Bible does not use the word "Trinity" as we have just used. So why then does it form the structure of the Creed? Why is it the presupposition of the Creed? Why is it so central to the faith? Why have orthodox Christians affirmed it for 2,000 years as the essence of Christianity?

It is important to see that, although the Bible does not teach the doctrine of the Trinity in so many words, the Bible teaches truths that cannot be understood without the doctrine of the Trinity. By this I mean that, although the doctrine of the Trinity was first put into words and taught in the third and fourth centuries, it is also true to say that the development of this doctrine was an inevitable result of taking the Bible seriously.

Let me try to shed more light on this claim. If you take the Bible seriously, you have a great deal of respect for a central theme in Old Testament revelation—namely, that there is only one true God and all the other so-called gods are really just idols or demons masquerading as gods. Listen to a creed known as the Shema, from early Israelite religion:

> Hear, O Israel: The LORD our God, the Lord is one. You shall love the LORD your God with all your heart and with all your soul and with all your might (Deuteronomy 6:4–5).

The prophets continually called on Israel to forsake idolatry and to worship only God, that is, to love the LORD with all their heart and soul and strength as the Shema commands. We call this "monotheism," the belief in only one God. The people of Israel repeatedly committed idolatry, until, after many prophetic warnings, God finally brought catastrophe upon them: Jerusalem was destroyed, the Temple was destroyed, the monarchy was destroyed, the people went off into captivity in Babylon and all hope seemed to be lost.

But prophets like Isaiah gave Israel hope and, sure enough, the nation was not allowed to perish completely. There was a return from captivity, a rebuilding of the Temple and the reestablishment of the covenant community under Ezra and Nehemiah. From then on, gross forms of idolatry were no longer a temptation for Israel.

Given all this history, the New Testament apostles could hardly repudiate the teaching on monotheism and still claim to be Jews. The whole Old Testament would have to be thrown out. Yet it was precisely the Old Testament that served to vindicate the apostles' claim that Jesus was the long-awaited Messiah, the Son of God.

The apostles were convinced that in the person of Jesus, God had come among them in the flesh:

> In the beginning was the Word, and the Word was with God, and the Word was God (John 1:1).

The apostles were convinced that his astonishing claims to divinity were true and Jesus was divine. This became the core of their preaching and the basis of the gospel they took from Jerusalem to Judea and Samaria and to the uttermost parts of the earth.

3. The doctrine of the Trinity is a mystery.

So the doctrine of the Trinity is a way of specifying that we must hold two basic beliefs together: *the oneness of God (monotheism)* and *the deity of Jesus Christ*. (Gradually the deity of the Holy Spirit was seen as a further implication of the deity of Christ and the existence within the one God of plurality.) The doctrine of the Trinity is a guide to what we can say and not say about God while managing to avoid denying either of these two essential truths. It is a mystery because it is a *paradox*, not a contradiction. In a contradiction, we assert two logically opposite truths at once, whereas in a paradox, we assert two truths that *appear* to be contradictory, but are not necessarily so, because we do not fully understand what they mean. God is a mystery beyond our understanding, not a self-contradictory concept.

Some critics of Christianity complain that the doctrine of the Trinity does not explain how God can be one and three at the same time. But they misunderstand. The doctrine of the Trinity does not claim to be capable of *explaining* this mystery. The oneness and threeness of God is not something that our finite, human minds are capable of understanding totally. We can understand that God is both one and three, but we can never understand *how* this is so.

This should not be seen as a defect in Christianity. If God was capable of fitting within our finite understanding, he would necessarily then be finite as we are. And if God were finite, he would not be the God of the Bible. The God of the Bible is the infinite, personal, Creator God. He is not comprehensible by us. He is knowable to us because he makes himself known. But even as we know him, we do not comprehend him.

This should not be a difficult thing for us to grasp, however. Even on the human interpersonal level, we know other human beings and yet we never completely know them. Even a husband and wife, who know each other more intimately and completely than any other person knows either of them, can still be learning new things about the other person after thirty years of marriage. If knowing another human being comprehensively is so difficult, how easy it should be for us to understand that it is completely impossible for any of us to know God so well that we fully comprehend who and what he is in the depths of his being.

And yet, because Jesus is not just a replica or a picture or a creature of God, but very God of very God, we can have perfect confidence that once we know Jesus, we really do know God. You do not have to comprehend someone fully in order to trust him or her. You just have to know him or her truly. And through Jesus Christ we do know God *truly*. That is the basis for our confidence in God and our hope for eternal life.

CONCLUSION

The doctrine of the Trinity is the core of the Christian faith. It is what makes Christianity unique. No one can be a Christian without believing this doctrine because to deny it is to fashion a god in one's own image who is not the God of the Bible. We believe in God the Father, God the Son and God the Holy Spirit, three persons, one being.

When Jesus appeared to his disciples for the final time, as described in Matthew 28, he said:

> All authority in heaven and on earth has been given to me. Go therefore and make disciples of all nations, baptizing them in the name of the Father and of the Son and of the Holy Spirit, teaching them to observe all that I have commanded you. And behold, I am with you always, to the end of the age (Matthew 28:18–20).

In the act of baptism, the church separates those who wish to be Jesus' disciples from the world and incorporates them into the body of Christ, the church. In this passage, Jesus commands us to baptize in the threefold name of the Father, the Son and the Holy Spirit because the only way to be saved is through the triune God. Surely this allows us to see the centrality of belief in the triune God. To believe in this God is to be a disciple of Jesus, a child of God, a Christian. It is through the triune Name that one enters into salvation. To believe in the triune God is eternal life. Not to believe is to stand outside the church and outside of salvation.

Questions for reflection

1. What are some gods that are worshipped by people you know personally other than the God of the Bible?

2. Summarize the biblical narrative as it is given in the Apostles' Creed.

3. How would you respond to a person who objects to the doctrine of the Trinity by stating that this doctrine is not taught in Scripture?

5

What does the first article of the Apostles' Creed teach us?

PART II
The Bible and the Apostles' Creed—God the Father
QUESTIONS 12-14

"The first article tells us that the Creator of the universe
is also our loving Father."

INTRODUCTION

Who is God? The Christian answer, as taught in the Bible, is: *God is the immutable, perfect, all-powerful, First Cause of the universe who speaks and acts in history to create, love and save his people.* This is what makes the Christian notion of God absolutely unique in the world. No other religion, philosophy, culture, ideology or movement has a conception of God like this one.

Other religions have conceptions of God as absolute power, like Islam, but while Allah acts benevolently to his people, it is by no means certain that he is benevolent to other people or that he is bound by his very nature always to be benevolent even to his own people. Therefore, Muslims live in a holy fear of Allah. But as John says: "Perfect love drives out fear." The context of this statement is:

God is love, and whoever abides in love abides in God, and God abides in him. By this is love perfected with us, so that we may have confidence for the day of judgment, because as he is so also are we in this world. There is no fear in love, but perfect love casts out fear. For fear has to do with punishment, and whoever fears has not been perfected in love (1 John 4:16–18).

The Christian God is love and to know this is to realize that his love for us is not temporary, accidental or conditional.

QUESTION 12: What does it mean to call God "Father"?

It means that God is not an impersonal force, but a real, living, loving person who made me and cares about me (Matthew 6:26).

This question and answer reminds us that Jesus revolutionized the concept of God by referring to God as his *Father*. A father is not a force or a principle, but rather, a person to whom we are related. When Scripture tells us to fear God, the meaning of fear is actually reverence. We revere and bless the name of God. But we need not fear that he will suddenly turn on us and destroy us on a whim. That is not his nature.

Other religions have conceptions of gods who are loving and benevolent, but not omnipotent. The Greeks, in their pantheon of gods, for example, had certain ones that were very well-disposed toward humans. For example, in Virgil's great poem *The Aeneid*, the goddess Venus shows special concern and love for the hero Aeneas, but her power is limited by the power and influence of the other gods, some of whom were bitterly hateful of Aeneas, including Juno, the wife of the king of the gods, Jupiter. Aeneas could count on Venus' love and solicitude for his wellbeing, but he had to recognize that her power was limited and could only extend so far. So, the believer in the Greek gods, like a Muslim, though for different reasons, had to live in fear as well.

Perhaps it is going too far to say that the believer in other gods must live in fear all the time. Nevertheless, it remains true that followers of gods other than the God of the Bible can have no confidence that their god is both all-powerful and all-loving at the same time. By contrast, this is the heart and soul and uniqueness of the Christian faith, and it is why everyone in the world needs to hear the gospel.

I. THE ATTRIBUTES OF GOD AND THE CHARACTER OF GOD

When Christian theology moved out into the wider ancient world during the missionary outreach of the church during the first few centuries, it encountered Greek philosophy. In Greek philosophy, the idea of God had been much discussed, and philosophers had developed various lists of attributes of the divine being.

QUESTION 13: What does it mean to call God the "almighty"?

It means that God is all-powerful and the sovereign Lord of the universe. Therefore he is able to watch over us and to guide all things by his providence. Nothing can snatch us out of his hand (John 10:28–30) and no power can separate us from the love of God that is in Christ Jesus (Romans 8:39).

Some of the Greek philosophers conceived God as timeless, unchanging, omnipotent, self-sufficient, unmoving and complete in himself. Greek philosophers like Plato and Aristotle had reacted against the popular religion of the Greek gods like Zeus, Venus and the rest. These popular gods were little more than very powerful human beings with all the weaknesses and shortcomings typical of human beings. They ate, drank, had sexual relations with one another and constantly feuded with each other. They were jealous, petty and liable to change their minds arbitrarily. So you can see why the philosophers might be inclined to be skeptical about the gods of popular Greek religion and to dismiss them as unworthy even to be called "gods." The Greek philosophers therefore conceived of god as the polar opposite of these popular deities: as eternal, unchanging, impassive, all-powerful, and so on.

When Christian missionaries took the gospel into this culture, they faced these questions: Do we present the God of the Bible as being basically like the god of the philosophers or do we take pains to distinguish him from the god of the philosophers? And, if we distinguish the God of the Bible from the god of the philosophers, will people then view our God as just another one of these petty deities and have no respect for him at all? Remember, this was the late Greco-Roman period, and many educated people no longer believed in the popular Greek gods. But the Bible seemed to early Christians to be quite clear on this point. In addition to God being our personal Father, God is nothing like the petty, limited gods of Greco-Roman religion. The God of the Bible is clearly almighty.

So how did early Christian pastors and evangelists deal with this dilemma? If they portrayed the God of the Bible in philosophical terms, they ran the risk of people thinking that the Christian God is just an impersonal force like Aristotle's "Unmoved Mover." But if they portrayed the God of the Bible in more personal terms, they ran the risk of people thinking of the Christian God as a petty, jealous, limited deity (who likely did not exist), just like the gods of popular Greek religion. In the end, they refused to compromise the biblical concept of God in either direction. They proclaimed God as "the Father almighty," meaning that God is *both* the personal God who speaks and acts in history in judgement and salvation *and also, at the same time*, the immutable, perfect, all-powerful First Cause of the universe.

A complicating factor was that the Bible speaks of God in many places in terms similar to those used in Greek philosophy. God is portrayed as all-knowing, all-powerful, unchanging and eternal. But the Bible also portrays God in very personal terms as loving, longsuffering, patient, merciful and gracious. As the Creed reminds us, God is our Father.

What would you have done in that situation? Gradually, early Christian theologians, pastors and preachers became clear about the fact that, although God is beyond time and space and eternally unchanging in his being, God has also revealed himself in history and acted in a personal way to enter into a relationship with us, first with Israel, and then climactically with both Jew and Gentile in the person of Jesus Christ.

So we have to view God in personal terms insofar as he acts in history, but we must always remember that God is not a being *within* the physical, space-time universe but rather the sovereign *Creator* of that universe. He is both *immanent* (active within our universe) and *transcendent* (beyond and not contained within our universe).

One way to put it is to say that in God's self-revelation in history, climaxing in Jesus Christ, we see the *character* of God displayed. And the character of God is rooted in the *attributes* of God, as he is beyond time and space in eternity. And unlike anything in ancient Greek religion, the Bible makes a *link* between the personal God speaking and acting in history and the almighty God beyond the universe. This link is made specifically in the incarnation of the second person of the Trinity, the Word became flesh. Because God has become flesh in the person of Jesus Christ, we can have confidence that God really is a personal union of infinite power and absolute goodness. With this background in mind, let us turn to Isaiah 40.

II. THE DEPICTION OF GOD IN ISAIAH 40

This chapter is a prophecy addressed to Israel at the time of the Babylonian captivity. The people of God have been in exile for seventy years because of their idolatry and oppression of the poor, just as the prophets had predicted. But now, the voice of the prophet cries out good news: the exile is almost over. God is about to bring his people back home. Deliverance is at hand. Israel's sin has been paid for and her punishment is now at an end.

The exodus from Egypt, the return from exile, the resurrection and the second coming of Christ are four key or hinge moments in salvation history when God acts decisively to bring redemption to his people. This coming return of the people to the Promised Land is treated as a second exodus— this time from Babylon instead of Egypt. Just as the original exodus was a complex series of events marked by the dramatic intervention of the mighty arm of the LORD, so now also the prophet Isaiah describes the imminent return in dramatic, supernatural terms.

Let us note carefully that this passage teaches twelve important truths about God:

1. God is faithful to his people, even when his people rebel against him.

This magnificent chapter opens with the cry, which I cannot read without having the awe-inspiring music from Handel's *Messiah* running through my head:

> Comfort ye, comfort ye my people, saith your God. Speak ye comfortably to Jerusalem, and cry unto her, that her warfare is accomplished, that her iniquity is pardoned: for she hath received of the LORD's hand double for all her sins (Isaiah 40:1–2 KJV).

For the exiles in captivity in Babylon this was the greatest news they could possibly hope to hear, and it was in response to their greatest fear, namely, that God had abandoned them forever. The prophetic message is that God has not forgotten his people, God has not abandoned them permanently, Yahweh is still their God. The Bible teaches that, while humans are fickle and undependable, God is faithful to his Word, faithful to his promise, faithful to his covenant and faithful to his chosen people.

2. God glorifies himself by displaying his graciousness to the whole creation as he brings salvation to his undeserving people.

> A voice cries:
> "In the wilderness prepare the way of the LORD;
>   make straight in the desert a highway for our God.
> Every valley shall be lifted up,
>   and every mountain and hill be made low;
> the uneven ground shall become level,

and the rough places a plain.
And the glory of the LORD shall be revealed,
   and all flesh shall see it together,
   for the mouth of the LORD has spoken" (Isaiah 40:3–5).

This great act of deliverance of God's people from captivity in Babylon is described here in poetic terms as a triumphant procession in which God leads his people through the wilderness separating Babylon and the land of Israel. The whole world is supposed to see the mighty act of God by which the people of Israel are preserved and delivered.

When the Holy Roman Emperor, Frederick the Great (1194–1250), asked a theologian in his court for a proof of the existence of God, the theologian is supposed to have replied: "The Jews, sire, the Jews." And indeed, the very existence of this people today after 4,000 years of Satanic attacks on them is an amazing indicator of the providential protection of an infinite, personal, Creator God.

3. God's Word stands forever because, unlike mortal people, he is eternal.

A voice says, "Cry!"
   And I said, "What shall I cry?"
All flesh is grass,
   and all its beauty is like the flower of the field.
The grass withers, the flower fades
   when the breath of the LORD blows on it;
   surely the people are grass.
The grass withers, the flower fades,
   but the word of our God will stand forever (Isaiah 40:6–8).

God's word brought creation into being: "In the beginning was the Word.... All things were made through him.... And God said, 'Let there be light,' and there was light" (John 1:1,3; Genesis 1:3). God's word of judgement will be pronounced on the last day of this creation before all comes to an end and the new heavens and the new earth come into being. God's Word stands forever. We are but a shadow, but God is eternal.

4. God is the all-powerful Lord who can do whatever he wills.

Go on up to a high mountain,
   O Zion, herald of good news;
lift up your voice with strength,
   O Jerusalem, herald of good news;

lift it up, fear not;
say to the cities of Judah,
   "Behold your God!"
Behold, the LORD God comes with might,
   and his arm rules for him;
behold, his reward is with him,
   and his recompense before him (Isaiah 40:9–10).

God's power over all the kingdoms of this world was displayed in the Babylonian Captivity. God allowed Babylon to conquer Israel only because Israel had to be punished for her disobedience. But then God allowed Persia to conquer Babylon because Babylon had to be punished for attacking God's people. Then God caused Cyrus, king of Persia, to grant permission for his people to be restored to their land. All the ups and downs of world history are under God's sovereign control. The rise and fall of the Roman Empire, the British Empire, the Soviet Empire and the American Empire—all are under his sovereignty.

5. God is a gentle shepherd who cares for his flock, despite his awesome power and strength.

He will tend his flock like a shepherd;
   he will gather the lambs in his arms;
he will carry them in his bosom,
   and gently lead those that are with young (Isaiah 40:11).

This God, who made the universe and who acts sovereignly in history to accomplish his will, is also a gentle, caring shepherd who loves and cares for his flock. The poet who wrote this passage shows tremendous artistry in placing such contrasts together. The all-powerful One is also gentle.

6. God's infinity is beyond our comprehension.
If the reader is wondering how such an all-powerful God can be such a gentle and caring shepherd, the next verse reminds us that we cannot be expected to comprehend our Maker:

Who has measured the waters in the hollow of his hand
   and marked off the heavens with a span,
enclosed the dust of the earth in a measure
   and weighed the mountains in scales
   and the hills in a balance? (Isaiah 40:12)

Of course, the answer to these rhetorical questions is "No one." We are limited, finite creatures, and we cannot possibly hope to comprehend the personal, infinite Creator God. We would know nothing true about him if he had not revealed himself to us.

7. God's mind is so much greater than our finite minds that he is all-knowing.

> Who has measured the Spirit of the LORD,
>   or what man shows him his counsel?
> Whom did he consult,
>   and who made him understand?
> Who taught him the path of justice,
>   and taught him knowledge,
>   and showed him the way of understanding? (Isaiah 40:13–14)

God knows everything past, present and future. Every moment of time is the eternal present to him. There are some things we do not know and cannot know because no creature could ever know them. Only an infinite mind can know some things, and only God has an infinite mind.

8. God is the Lord of the nations, which are nothing in comparison to him.

> Behold, the nations are like a drop from a bucket,
>   and are accounted as the dust on the scales;
>   behold, he takes up the coastlands like fine dust.
> Lebanon would not suffice for fuel,
>   nor are its beasts enough for a burnt offering.
> All the nations are as nothing before him,
>   they are accounted by him as less than nothing and emptiness
> (Isaiah 40:15–17).

God is the LORD of the nations. As we noted earlier, he controls world history, allowing one king to conquer another and then deciding when the conquering king will in turn fall. No human power can stand up to the LORD.

9. God is the living God and totally unlike all the idols, which are mere inanimate objects.

> To whom then will you liken God,
>   or what likeness compare with him?
> An idol! A craftsman casts it,
>   and a goldsmith overlays it with gold

and casts for it silver chains.
He who is too impoverished for an offering
    chooses wood that will not rot;
he seeks out a skillful craftsman
    to set up an idol that will not move (Isaiah 40:18–20).

God is the living God, not a dead idol. As a living God, God speaks through the mouth of his prophets. He acts in history to deliver his people. He hears the cries of those in bondage and responds with an act of gracious mercy. He is alive. He loves, he judges, he is not deaf and dumb.

10. God is the sovereign Lord of history who dictates the affairs of the earth from his heavenly throne.

Do you not know? Do you not hear?
    Has it not been told you from the beginning?
    Have you not understood from the foundations of the earth?
It is he who sits above the circle of the earth,
    and its inhabitants are like grasshoppers;
who stretches out the heavens like a curtain,
    and spreads them like a tent to dwell in;
who brings princes to nothing,
    and makes the rulers of the earth as emptiness.
Scarcely are they planted, scarcely sown,
    scarcely has their stem taken root in the earth,
when he blows on them, and they wither,
    and the tempest carries them off like stubble (Isaiah 40:21–24).

God is in control of history. History is going somewhere. It is going toward the kingdom of God. Of course, from our vantage point, that is not usually obvious. Only by faith can we make this assertion. Our faith that history has meaning rests on our faith in the Lord of history.

11. God is the incomparable Creator of the heavens and the earth.

To whom then will you compare me,
    that I should be like him? says the Holy One.
Lift up your eyes on high and see:
    who created these?
He who brings out their host by number,
    calling them all by name;
by the greatness of his might

> and because he is strong in power,
>   not one is missing (Isaiah 40:25–26).

God is Lord of history precisely because he is the Creator of the universe. He is not part of the universe, trapped by its laws and limited by space and time. No, he is the One who spoke and the worlds came into being. He upholds creation by his Word and can act into it at any time.

12. God is the Saviour of his people who put their hope in him.

> Why do you say, O Jacob,
>   and speak, O Israel,
> "My way is hidden from the LORD,
>   and my right is disregarded by my God"?
> Have you not known? Have you not heard?
> The LORD is the everlasting God,
>   the Creator of the ends of the earth.
> He does not faint or grow weary;
>   his understanding is unsearchable.
> He gives power to the faint,
>   and to him who has no might he increases strength.
> Even youths shall faint and be weary,
>   and young men shall fall exhausted;
> but they who wait for the LORD shall renew their strength;
>   they shall mount up with wings like eagles;
> they shall run and not be weary;
>   they shall walk and not faint (Isaiah 40:27–31).

We are always tempted, as the children of Israel were during the Babylonian captivity, to give up on God. We are tempted to complain that God has forgotten us. In our misery, we often betray our self-centredness and our lack of faith. But here the prophet, in a moving and powerful way, assures us that God is the Saviour of his people. He gives strength to the weak. He saves those who call upon his name. He is the Saviour.

III. THE ATTRIBUTES AND CHARACTER OF GOD IN ISAIAH 40

This passage contains a mixture of what one might call the *attributes* of God, that is, aspects of his eternal being as he is in himself: eternal, infinite, all-powerful, and so on. But it also contains descriptions of the *character* of God, that is, aspects of his character as revealed by his actions in history: faithful, gracious, Saviour. Furthermore, this passage grounds the revealed character of God in the attributes of God as he is in himself beyond all space and time. This is what makes the message of the Bible powerful, unique and such good news. When we prayerfully meditate on these twelve truths, we can see that:

1. God is *eternal* (6–8), and the expression of his character is *faithfulness* (1–2).
2. God is *infinite* (12), and the expression of his character is *graciousness* (3–5).
3. God is *all-powerful* (9–10), and the expression of his character is his *creation of the world* (25–26).
4. God is *all-knowing* (13–14), and the expression of his character is his *sovereignty* in history (21–24).
5. God is *alive* (18–20), and the expression of his character is to be the LORD *of the nations* (15–17).
6. God is *gentle* (11), and the expression of his character is to be the *Saviour* (27–31).

IV. WHAT IT MEANS TO BE CREATED IN THE IMAGE OF THIS GOD

This concept of God is unique; the God of the Bible is both the eternal, all-powerful, all-knowing, sovereign Creator of the universe and, *at the same time*, the faithful, gracious LORD and Saviour of the world. He is the First Cause of the universe as the philosophers rightly discerned, but he is also the one who answers prayer, does miracles and intervenes in history to save his people. He is both *transcendent* and *immanent* at the same time. He is the triune God: Father, Son and Holy Spirit.

QUESTION 14: What does it mean to call God the "creator of heaven and earth"?

It means that God is the creator of all things visible and invisible as taught in the Holy Scriptures (Genesis 1–2; Psalm 19:1–6; Isaiah 42:5). As creator, God has made man in his own image, as male and female (Genesis 1:26–27). Thus, we are blessed to have our loving, heavenly Father as our creator, and we are doubly blessed to be created in his image.

It is important to understand that *this* is the God in whose image we have been created. Question 14 asks what it means to call God "creator of the heaven and the earth," and in the answer we learn it means, first, that God has created the totality of reality out of nothing (Genesis 1:1). Secondly, it means that God had made man in his own image as male and female (Genesis 1:26–27). This means that we have the creator of all things as our loving, heavenly Father, and it also means that we have been created in his image.

The nineteenth-century atheist Ludwig Feuerbach claimed that God is a projection of a "father figure" upon the sky. We feel unsafe in a dangerous and unpredictable world, so we invent an "imaginary friend" who is just like us, only bigger and stronger. But if that were the case, then we would have invented a God who was less mysterious and more like us. The God of the Bible is not a human writ large; the God of the Bible is a mysterious and transcendent deity, and it is we who resemble him in certain (but not all) ways, rather than he resembling us.

CONCLUSION

There is a children's prayer that goes like this: "God is great, God is good. Let us thank him for our food. Amen." This is short and sweet! But what a tremendous summary of the nature of the Christian God this little prayer contains. The Christian God is neither power without goodness nor goodness without power; God is not arbitrary, all-powerful, sheer will, nor is he goodness lacking in power to put his will into effect. Rather, God is all-loving and all-powerful at the same time. The greatness of God and the goodness of God come together in one Being.

At the beginning of this study, I offered this definition of God: *God is the immutable, perfect, all-powerful First Cause of the universe who speaks and acts in history to create, love and save his people.* The child's grace is a shorter and simpler version of this theological definition! Isn't that amazing! Look at the chart (opposite), which connects this simple prayer to the definition using attributes and characteristics from Isaiah 40.

The truth about God is so profound that it is simple enough for a child to learn and understand, while at the same time being beyond the ability of the greatest and most learned theologian to fully comprehend. This is our God!

THE ATTRIBUTES OF GOD IN ISAIAH 40

GOD IS GREAT Attributes of power	GOD IS GOOD Attributes of goodness
Eternal (6–8)	Faithful (1–2)
Infinite (12)	Gracious (3–5)
All-powerful (9–10)	Creator (25–26)
All-knowing (13–14)	Sovereign Lord of history (21–24)
Living (18–20)	Lord of the nations (15–17)
Gentle (11)	Saviour (27–31)

Questions for reflection

1. How did Jesus revolutionize the concept of God?

2. What dilemma did the early Christian preachers and theologian face when it came to speaking about God?

3. Have you ever heard God described in ways that make him seem like one of the Greek gods, that is, as a being in the universe only bigger and stronger than us?

4. How would the exiles in Babylon likely have responded to the depiction of God contained in Isaiah 40?

5. Identify some ways in which the biblical God is incomprehensible?

6

What does the second article of the Apostles' Creed teach us?

PART II
The Bible and the Apostles' Creed—God the Son
QUESTIONS 15-23

"The second article tells us that Jesus Christ died
and rose again for our salvation."

INTRODUCTION

When we come to the second article of the Apostles' Creed, we come to the second person of the Trinity, God the Son, Jesus Christ. It is no accident that the second article is the longest of the three and that it is in the form of a narrative. Jesus Christ is the heart of Christian faith, and everything else we believe rests on the saving events recounted in the Gospels concerning his birth, life, death, resurrection, ascension and second coming. It is not accidental that the name of our faith is Christianity because Christ is at the centre of everything we hope for, everything we believe and everything we love. So we come to the most important question any person can ever ask, "Who is Jesus?"

> **QUESTION 15:** Who is Jesus Christ?
>
> Jesus Christ is revealed by Scripture to be the fulfilment of Israel's messianic hope as the Son of Man and the Son of God, and also as the King of kings and Lord of lords. This means that he is the God-Man, one person, fully divine and fully human, the second person of the Trinity.

In this chapter we cannot cover every important doctrine concerning Jesus Christ adequately. Our focus will be on the *person* of Christ, and we will be able to give only brief attention to the *work* of Christ. To know Jesus Christ and grasp who he truly is involves placing our faith in him as our Lord and Saviour; the one who does not do this can never know him in the intimate and personal way that believers do. To such an unbeliever, Jesus Christ will forever remain an enigma. But the person who believes becomes a child of God:

> But to all who did receive him, who believed in his name, he gave the right to become children of God (John 1:12).

We cannot recognize as a fellow Christian anyone who does not believe in Jesus Christ. John writes:

> Beloved, do not believe every spirit, but test the spirits to see whether they are from God, for many false prophets have gone out into the world. By this you know the Spirit of God: every spirit that confesses that Jesus Christ has come in the flesh is from God, and every spirit that does not confess Jesus is not from God (1 John 4:1–3).

In the early church some people could not believe that God really became an actual human being. This passage says that such people are not really Christians. In the modern age, it is more common for people to say they cannot believe that Jesus was really God come in the flesh. But the New Testament teaches both truths: *Jesus Christ is fully man and fully God, one person with two natures.*

I. THE HUMANITY OF JESUS CHRIST

The Bible clearly teaches the real humanity of Jesus Christ. Let us note seven things Scripture teaches about the humanity of Jesus.

1. He was born of a woman.

> And Joseph also went up from Galilee, from the town of Nazareth, to Judea, to the city of David, which is called Bethlehem, because he was of the house and lineage of David, to be registered with Mary, his betrothed, who was with child. And while they were there, the time came for her to give birth. And she gave birth to her firstborn son (Luke 2:4–7).

Only his conception was supernatural. He was born like any other baby of an ordinary woman. Jesus was really a normal baby who cried like anyone else, despite the line in the beautiful Christmas carol, "Silent Night," which says "Little Lord Jesus, no crying he makes." The catechism clarifies exactly what Scripture teaches with regard to the birth of Jesus and the significance of the virgin birth.

QUESTION 16: What does it mean when it says he was "conceived by the Holy Spirit"?

It means that his human body and soul were created by a miracle in which the Word took on human flesh by becoming incarnate in the man Jesus.

QUESTION 17: What is the significance of the virgin birth?

It means that the conception of Christ was a divine miracle, which makes Jesus both fully human, with a human mother, and fully divine, without a human father.

The virgin birth is not just a sign of Christ's divinity, which is how we usually think of it, but also of his humanity. He was born into the world from a human mother and so was actually and fully human.

2. He grew up like anyone else.

> And Jesus increased in wisdom and in stature and in favor with God and man (Luke 2:52).

Jesus also grew up like anyone else. He had normal intellectual, physical and social growth. He went through puberty and experienced all the usual phases of normal human development.

3. He experienced hunger and thirst.

And after fasting forty days and forty nights, he was hungry (Matthew 4:2).

Jesus experienced the usual human limitations of living in space and time. He got hungry and thirsty just like anyone else.

4. He grew tired when he travelled.

So he came to a town of Samaria called Sychar, near the field that Jacob had given to his son Joseph. Jacob's well was there; so Jesus, wearied as he was from his journey, was sitting beside the well. It was about the sixth hour (John 4:5–6).

He also got tired on long trips, just as you or I would do. He did not have omnipotence in his humanity.

5. He suffered pain.

And he began to teach them that the Son of Man must suffer many things and be rejected by the elders and the chief priests and the scribes and be killed, and after three days rise again (Mark 8:31).

Jesus suffered pain like anyone else and had as much incentive as you or I to avoid it.

QUESTION 18: What is the significance of mentioning his suffering under Pontius Pilate?

This means that Jesus was a real, historical figure who died at a certain historical time during the period of the Roman Empire when Pilate was governor of Judea. This is not just a fictional story with a moral; it is history.

Pilate is the only person other than Jesus who is named in the Creed. The apostles are not named, Mary is not named—only the Roman governor who condemned Jesus to death is named. Why? The point of mentioning

Pilate is to root the events in history. Pilate was a well-known Roman official of his time, and the Creed wants to remind us, as Paul puts it in his speech before King Agrippa, "this has not been done in a corner" (Acts 26:26). Jesus suffered pain because he was really human, and it occurred under a real Roman governor at a point in dateable, real history because the incarnation was really historical.

6. He experienced human emotions such as anger, grief, loneliness and joy.
When the religious leaders tried to catch Jesus breaking the Sabbath law by healing someone in the synagogue, we are told in Mark 3:5, "And he looked around at them with anger, grieved at their hardness of heart, and said to the man, 'Stretch out your hand.' He stretched it out, and his hand was restored."

He also knew grief. We are told that when he stood before the tomb of Lazarus, "Jesus wept" (John 11:35). On the cross, Jesus experienced the most profound loneliness any human being could ever experience. He cries out: "'Eloi, Eloi, lema sabachthani?' which means, 'My God, my God, why have you forsaken me?'" (Mark 15:34). We are told in Hebrews 12 that Jesus was motivated to be faithful even to the point of dying on the cross in order to fulfil his mission "for the joy that was set before him" (Hebrews 12:2).

Jesus experienced the full range of human emotions. This is a reminder that such emotions are part of the way God made us and are not evil in themselves. Of course, emotions do open us up to temptation and create an opening that Satan can exploit in tempting us. Ephesians 4:26 says, "Be angry and do not sin," and in his anger, Jesus did not sin.

7. He did not know everything.
In Mark 13:32, Jesus says of his second coming: "But concerning that day or that hour, no one knows, not even the angels in heaven, nor the Son, but only the Father." In his incarnate state, Jesus voluntarily limited his power so as to experience fully what it means to be human. Those times when he had supernatural insight into what other people were thinking or into the future are examples of knowledge given to him by the Holy Spirit just as the Holy Spirit gave similar bits of special knowledge to various prophets throughout biblical history.

II. THE DEITY OF JESUS CHRIST

The Bible clearly teaches the real deity of Jesus Christ, which is also implied by his virgin birth. This was by no means an easy conclusion for the first disciples to accept. It went directly against the grain of their fervent

Jewish monotheism, and it clearly was every bit as mind boggling and hard to understand for them as it is for us today. Yet the testimony of the New Testament is plain and unified on this key point.

1. His pre-existence

The New Testament is clear that, although Jesus was born of the virgin Mary, this was not the beginning of his existence: "Truly, truly, I say to you, before Abraham was, I am." (John 8:58). The Word of God, which became joined to the human Jesus, is eternal, and so the person Jesus Christ is pre-existent. This is not to say that Jesus the man is eternal, but only to say that the Word is eternal. Yet Jesus Christ, the Son of God is one person with two natures, and therefore it is appropriate to speak of the pre-existence of Jesus Christ. As Question 16 puts it, his virginal conception was a miracle of the Holy Spirit in which the eternal Word, without ceasing to be the eternal Word, took on human flesh and became incarnate.

2. His virgin birth

Jesus was born of a virgin, which is to say that he was conceived in the womb of Mary by a supernatural act of God and had no human father in a physical sense. Joseph became his adopted father.

> Now the birth of Jesus Christ took place in this way. When his mother Mary had been betrothed to Joseph, before they came together she was found to be with child from the Holy Spirit (Matthew 1:18).

Jesus Christ was the promised seed of the woman who was prophesied in Genesis 3:15 as the one who would crush the head of the serpent.

3. His sinless life

The New Testament is very clear that Jesus was fully human, and even though he was severely tempted by Satan, he lived a sinless life. The account of his temptation is given in Matthew 4:1–11. Reflecting on this incident in the life of Jesus, the writer of Hebrews says:

> For we do not have a high priest who is unable to sympathize with our weaknesses, but one who in every respect has been tempted as we are, yet without sin (Hebrews 4:15).

This shows that human beings are not inherently sinful; they fell into sin. Sin is not part of what it means to be human—only part of what it means to be a member of Adam's fallen race. Jesus was tempted. To be tempted is not the same as sinning. Jesus experienced temptation in the same way as

Adam and Eve did, but the second Adam did not give in to temptation.

4. His astounding claims

Jesus made astonishing claims for himself. He claimed to be one with the Father (John10:30). He claimed to have the authority to forgive sins (Mark 2:10). He claimed that all judgement was given into his hands (John 5:27) and that on the last day he would be the one to raise the dead (John 5:25). The Jewish leaders and religious scholars clearly understood his claims to be claims to deity, and in their unbelief they reacted accordingly, accusing him of blasphemy and eventually seeking his death.

5. His mighty works

The New Testament records that Jesus backed up his claim to deity with many miracles and mighty works. He confronted Satan and cast out demons from those victimized by evil powers. He healed all types of sicknesses and diseases (Luke 7:21). He even raised the dead on at least three occasions. In John 11, we have the dramatic account of the raising of Lazarus. In Luke 7:11–17, we see the raising from the dead of the widow's son and, in Luke 8:40–56, we have the raising of the daughter of a synagogue ruler named Jarius. He displayed mastery over nature and did all the things the promised Messiah was supposed to do.

6. His atoning death

The New Testament teaches that Jesus' death on the cross was not an unfortunate accident; nor did it represent the failure of his mission. Instead, it portrays the death of Christ as the means by which the world is reconciled to God. Peter, preaching on the Day of Pentecost, says,

> this Jesus, delivered up according to the definite plan and foreknowledge of God, you crucified and killed by the hands of lawless men (Acts 2:23).

QUESTION 19: What is the significance of the phrase "was crucified, died and was buried"?

This emphasizes his substitutionary, propitiatory, atoning death on our behalf, which is the heart of the gospel (Romans 3:21–26).

Question 19 asks about the significance of Jesus' death on the cross. The answer is possibly the most complicated answer in the entire catechism. We need to go through it word by word.

His death was *substitutionary*. This means that Jesus was our substitute: "He himself bore our sins in his body on the tree" (1 Peter 2:24). Jesus was like the sacrificial animal in the Old Testament sacrificial system who was killed in place of the worshipper. We deserved death but he took our place and allowed himself to be killed in our stead. This is stressed over and over again in both the Old and New Testaments.

He death was *propitiatory*. To propitiate means to turn aside wrath. The death of Jesus in our place was accepted by the Father and deemed adequate to cover our sins, which meant that the wrath of the triune God was turned aside from us. Since Jesus took our place, he bore the wrath of a holy God instead of us having to bear it. He was the propitiation for our sins (1 John 2:2; 4:10) because God put him forward to be a propitiation for our sins (Romans 3:25). He was the high priest who made a propitiation for the sins of the people (Hebrews 2:17).

His death was *atoning*. This means that it provided atonement for sins that resulted in the restoration of fellowship between the holy God and sinful men and women. To atone is to "make one"—to bring two enemies together in reconciliation. This is the heart of the gospel—atonement by substitution and propitiation—and this is what the death of Christ achieved.

7. His bodily resurrection

Not only was the death of Jesus part of God's plan for the salvation of the world, but his resurrection from the dead by the power of God the Father vindicated him and made it clear to the world that he was the Son of God. Peter continues:

> God raised him up, loosing the pangs of death, because it was not possible for him to be held by it (Acts 2:24).

In 1 Corinthians 15:12–19, Paul emphatically states that the bodily resurrection of Jesus from the dead is perhaps *the* essential belief of the whole Christian faith. Paul says that this teaching was part of the basic gospel message he received from the Jerusalem apostles (1 Corinthians 15:4). If Christ is not risen then Paul says his preaching is vain (1 Corinthians 15:14) and Christian preachers, including Paul, are misrepresenting the facts of the matter and misleading people (15:15). Moreover, if Christ is not risen then the faith of Christians is in vain (15:14) and we are still in our sins (15:17). In addition, there is no hope for Christians who have died (15:18), and if Christian hope does not extend beyond this life then those who have suffered for their faith are to be pitied (15:19).

> **QUESTION 20:** What is the significance of the phrase "he descended to the dead"?
>
> ───
>
> It means two things. First, it means that Jesus really died on the cross. Second, it means that Jesus experienced death for us so that we might escape it (Acts 2:27).

"He descended to the dead" means two things: first, that Jesus really did die on the cross and, secondly, that he experienced death for us so that we could escape spiritual death. Death has no terror for the believer because Jesus has gone there ahead of us and we know that death cannot hold us in its grip.

> **QUESTION 21:** What is the significance of the phrase "On the third day he rose again"?
>
> ───
>
> This refers to the glorious and triumphant resurrection of our Lord from the dead by which he triumphed over death, hell and the devil (Romans 8:38–39).

This is our great and glorious hope. Our Lord's resurrection from the dead was the means by which he triumphed over death, hell and the devil. Without the resurrection, Christianity would be merely a beautiful story; with the resurrection, Christianity is not only beautiful but also true!

8. His glorious ascension

The New Testament also teaches that Jesus did not merely rise from the dead to die once more. Instead, he ascended into heaven to the right hand of the Father (the place of glory and authority) and reigns there now interceding on behalf of his witnesses here on earth.

> Then I turned to see the voice that was speaking to me, and on turning I saw seven golden lampstands, and in the midst of the lampstands one like a son of man, clothed with a long robe and with a golden sash around his chest. The hairs of his head were white, like white wool, like snow. His eyes were like a flame of fire, his feet were like burnished bronze, refined in a furnace, and his voice was like the roar of many waters. In his right hand he held seven stars, from his mouth came a sharp two-edged sword, and his face was like the sun shining in full

strength. When I saw him, I fell at his feet as though dead. But he laid his right hand on me, saying, "Fear not, I am the first and the last, and the living one. I died, and behold I am alive forevermore, and I have the keys of Death and Hades (Revelation 1:12–18).

QUESTION 22: What is the significance of the phrases "he ascended into heaven, he is seated at the right hand of the Father"?

After his resurrection, Jesus ascended to heaven until the end of this age when he will return. He is now alive and ruling at the right hand of the Father (Acts 7:56).

This section of the Apostles' Creed emphasizes that after his forty-day period of resurrection appearances, Jesus ascended to the right hand of the Father, the place of authority and rule (Acts 1:6–11). He is now alive and reigning from heaven over the entire cosmos. This world may look like it is out of control, and it may seem like the Devil is in full control, but by faith we know that this is not true because Jesus Christ reigns. One day every eye will see him and "every knee should bow, in heaven and on earth and under the earth, and every tongue confess that Jesus Christ is Lord, to the glory of God the Father" (Philippians 2:10–11).

9. His future return to earth

The New Testament teaches that at a future time, known only to the Father, Jesus will return from heaven to this earth. Whereas he came the first time as the suffering servant of Isaiah 53, then he will come as the conquering king of Isaiah 11. He will slay the wicked, set up the kingdom of God, judge the living and the dead and usher in the new heavens and the new earth.

Then I saw heaven opened, and behold, a white horse! The one sitting on it is called Faithful and True, and in righteousness he judges and makes war. His eyes are like a flame of fire, and on his head are many diadems, and he has a name written that no one knows but himself. He is clothed in a robe dipped in blood, and the name by which he is called is The Word of God. And the armies of heaven, arrayed in fine linen, white and pure, were following him on white horses. From his mouth comes a sharp sword with which to strike down the nations, and he will rule them with a rod of iron. He will tread the winepress of the fury of the wrath of God the Almighty. On his robe and on his thigh he has a name written, King of kings and Lord of lords (Revelation 19:11–16).

QUESTION 23: What is the significance of the phrases "he will come again to judge the living and the dead"?

It means that one day Jesus Christ will return to this earth in the same way as his disciples saw him leave when he ascended into heaven. This time he will come as conquering king, rather than as the suffering servant (Acts 1:11; 1 Thessalonians 4:13–18; Revelation 19:11–21).

This section speaks of the living hope of the church on earth: one day Jesus Christ will return to this earth in the same way the disciples saw him leave when he ascended into heaven. This time, however, he will come as the conquering king, not as the suffering servant. The New Testament promises that when he comes he will usher in events culminating in the day of judgement and the renewal of all things in the new heavens and new earth.

III. THE UNITY OF JESUS CHRIST

The Bible clearly teaches the unity of Jesus Christ as *one person with two natures*: a divine nature and a human nature united in one person. The language of persons and natures is, of course, not found in Scripture itself. The church developed these terms during the first four centuries after the New Testament period as pastors and theologians reflected on the biblical materials and tried to come with doctrinal formulations that would protect the church from various heresies.

The essential point that needs to be made is this: We must confess that Jesus Christ is fully divine and fully human *at the same time*. It wasn't that he was a man who *became* a god. This would not do justice to the New Testament. And he was not god while only *appearing* to be a man. We need to confess and believe that he is fully divine and fully human at the same time.

The best way to express this doctrine was debated for a long time. But in A.D. 451, a church council meeting at Chalcedon articulated the essence of the doctrine of the two natures of Christ with terminology that has since been accepted by nearly all Christians around the world. *The Definition of Chalcedon* did not try to *explain* how Jesus Christ is both fully God and fully man. No one could ever do that. Rather, what it did was to *define* clearly in terms as simple as possible exactly what one needs to believe on this point in order to be an orthodox Christian. Here is an exert from the statement containing the key terms:

We apprehend this one and only Christ—Son, Lord only-begotten—
in two natures; without confusing the two natures, without transmut-
ing one nature into the other, without dividing them into two separate
categories, without contrasting them according to area or function.
The distinctiveness of each nature is not nullified by the union.
Instead, the *properties* of each nature are conserved and both natures
concur in one *person* and in one *hypostasis*. They are not divided or cut
into two prosopa but are together the one and only and only-begotten
Logos of God, the Lord Jesus Christ. Thus have the prophets of old
testified; thus the Lord Jesus Christ himself taught us; thus the Symbol
of the Fathers has handed down.[1]

This doctrine is sometimes called the doctrine of the hypostatic union. It
means that we confess Jesus Christ to have two natures, one fully human
and one fully divine, united together in one person.

IV. THE IMPLICATIONS OF THIS DOCTRINE

It is important to stress that this doctrine is not a piece of irrelevant speculation, which ordinary believers can safely ignore. It is not a matter of
over-educated theologians with too much time on their hands making
Christianity way more complicated that it needs to be. This doctrine is
essential to our salvation, and it is a practical matter of spiritual life and
death to believe it.

Here are four concrete, practical implications, which follow directly
from the orthodox, biblical doctrine about Jesus Christ:

1. He is worthy of worship—the central act of the church.

Since Jesus Christ is fully divine, it is not wrong to worship him. We worship the human Jesus, and this would be idolatry if he were not one person
and also divine. The deity of Jesus Christ means that he is worthy of our
worship. He is even now being worshipped by thousands of angels in
heaven (Revelation 5:11–14).

2. He is able to save—our assurance of salvation.

Because Jesus is divine, he is able to save. He did not need to die for his
own sins on the cross, so he was able to die for *our* sins. And, because of
his divinity, his death was of infinite value in expiating sin. If he were not
divine, we would still be lost in our sins and without hope.

---

[1] Leith, *Creeds of the Churches*, 36.

3. He is the only Saviour of the world — the basis of world missions and evangelism.

As the fully human, fully divine God-Man, Jesus Christ is absolutely unique. "There is no other name under heaven given among men by which we must be saved" (Acts 4:12). As Baptists, this is the whole rationale behind our aggressive program of evangelism and world missions. If Jesus were not divine, it would be presumptuous to put him forward as the only Saviour of the world. If he is divine, it would be criminal not to do so.

4. He is trustworthy – the basis of our hope.

Because he is the divine Son of God, he is utterly trustworthy. We can safely put our hope in him and trust him in everything. Jesus said: "Believe in God; believe also in me" (John 14:1). We can do this because of who he is.

CONCLUSION

The doctrine of the person of Jesus Christ is that he is fully human and fully divine, one person with two natures. We cannot fully understand this doctrine, but we confess it as the only possible way to make sense of what God has revealed to us in the person of Jesus. We worship him and we bow before him. Unable to comprehend him, we nevertheless know him and love him as our Lord and Saviour. In the end we are left with a mystery to worship, not a puzzle to solve.

Questions for reflection

1. Can someone deny the incarnation and be a real Christian? What Bible verse is the basis for your answer?

2. What are seven lines of evidence given in the New Testament for the full humanity of Jesus Christ?

3. What are eight lines of evidence given in the New Testament for the full deity of Jesus Christ?

4. What is the doctrine of the hypostatic union?

5. What are some practical implications of the biblical and orthodox doctrine of Christ for the church and our daily lives?

7

What does the third article of the Apostles' Creed teach us?

PART II
The Bible and the Apostles' Creed—God the Holy Spirit
QUESTIONS 24–27

"The third article tells us that the Holy Spirit is redeeming the fallen creation.

INTRODUCTION

We now come to the third article of the Apostles' Creed. The first article of the creed focused on God the Father and the work of creation. The second article focused on God the Son, Jesus Christ, and the work of reconciliation. The third article focuses on God the Holy Spirit and the application of salvation in redemption.

We have seen that the Apostles' Creed is a reliable guide to the interpretation of the Bible because it is a summary of the Bible that arises out of the Bible itself as it was preached by the apostles of Jesus Christ. The first article of the creed grounds the whole creed in the Old Testament by affirming that the God of the Bible is the God who created the heavens and the earth. The second article of the creed, the longest, zeros in on the Gospels and their accounts of the life, death and resurrection of Jesus Christ. It identifies Jesus Christ with the God of the Old Testament. The third article speaks of the person and work of the Holy Spirit in the church, in the salvation of sinners and in the consummation of all things, which we see in Acts and the New Testament epistles. It tells us that the Holy Spirit applies the salvation won by Christ to the individual through the church's ministry and brings all things to their appointed final end.

I. I BELIEVE IN THE HOLY SPIRIT

The first part of the third article is a confession of our faith in the Holy Spirit.

QUESTION 24: What does it mean to "believe in the Holy Spirit"?

It means that we believe that the Holy Spirit is fully divine, the third person of the Godhead. The Spirit fills and empowers us for service as we strive to do God's will (Acts 2:4; Romans 8:26–29; Galatians 5:16–18).

There is a lot of misunderstanding regarding the Holy Spirit today. First, in the Roman Catholic Church there is an unfortunate tendency to box the Spirit in by saying that the Spirit can only work through the sacraments of the Roman church as administered by the sacramental priesthood. This limits the Holy Spirit to the boundaries of a human institution. But the Reformation taught that the Spirit could work through any person or movement he wants because he is free and sovereign. As Jesus said to Nicodemus, "The wind blows where it wishes, and you hear its sound, but you do not know where it comes from or where it goes. So it is with everyone who is born of the Spirit" (John 3:8).

Second, in the older, historic Protestant denominations there is a deplorable lack of awareness of the person and work of the Holy Spirit due to the influence of liberal theology, which tends to reduce the Holy Spirit to a mere force or vague influence—that makes the Holy Spirit into a mysterious, impersonal force, off somewhere doing who knows what. It is easy to see how people brought up on this sort of thing could watch *Star Wars* movies and think that the Christian Holy Spirit is something like the Force.

Third, in an understandable reaction to the Roman Catholic and liberal Protestant tendencies to box in or ignore the Spirit, many Christians in Pentecostal churches and the Charismatic movement get so wrapped up in talking about the Holy Spirit and the various manifestations of the activity of the Holy Spirit—in the form of miracles, emotional outbursts, signs and wonders and speaking in tongues—that they sometimes end up neglecting Jesus. Yet Jesus said that the Holy Spirit, when he comes, would testify to him and bring glory to him (John 15:26).

Another danger for Pentecostal and charismatic Christians is that they can emphasize *experience* to the point of forgetting that we live by *faith*. For example, our assurance of salvation is rooted in God's Word and the death and resurrection of Jesus Christ, not in how spiritual we happen to feel on a particular day. Also, if you over-emphasize experience you can end up putting your own experience above the Word of God as the highest theological authority. This can lead to heresy and spiritual problems of many kinds. This is classical theological liberalism—the very type of theology that minimizes the doctrine of the Holy Spirit. The only way to have a sound, balanced doctrine of the Holy Spirit is to go to Scripture, not Hollywood movies, and to let our experience be shaped and moulded by what the Scripture teaches about the person and work of the Holy Spirit.

There are many evangelical Christians who live their lives as though the Holy Spirit does not even exist. Their ignorance of the Spirit's ministry rivals that of the Ephesian converts described in Acts 19. When Paul came to Ephesus, it says that he found some disciples there and asked them if they had received the Holy Spirit when they believed. They replied, "No, we have not even heard that there is a Holy Spirit" (Acts 19:2). It turns out that they had been converted through the ministry of John the Baptist before the Day of Pentecost, so they at least, had a good excuse. But there is no good excuse for Christians today not to be alive to the reality and presence of the Holy Spirit in their lives.

What does the Holy Spirit do? We can divide the work of the Holy Spirit into parts for the sake of convenience: his work in the salvation of sinners and his work in the lives of believers.

A. THE WORK OF THE HOLY SPIRIT IN THE SALVATION OF SINNERS

The Holy Spirit does four things in the salvation of sinners:

1. The Holy Spirit brings us under conviction of sin.
Jesus said of the Holy Spirit:

> And when he comes, he will convict the world concerning sin and righteousness and judgment (John 16:8).

Anyone who has become a Christian knows what it means to come under conviction of sin. It seems that your eyes are opened, and you see the righteousness of God and sinfulness of your own life side by side. Once this happens, you realize instantly that you stand under the judgement of a wrathful God who cannot tolerate sin. You realize that nothing stands between you and the lake of fire. It is the Spirit of God who creates this awareness in us by opening our eyes, which previously were blinded by sin.

2. The Holy Spirit regenerates us and makes us alive in Christ.

Scripture speaks of the new birth as the work of the Father through the Son:

> Blessed be the God and Father of our Lord Jesus Christ! According to his great mercy, he has caused us to be born again to a living hope through the resurrection of Jesus Christ from the dead (1 Peter 1:3).

But Jesus told Nicodemus that no one enters the kingdom of God unless he or she is born again by the Spirit of God (John 3:3–8), so it is through the Holy Spirit, on the basis of the atonement of Jesus Christ, that God causes us to be born again.

3. The Holy Spirit baptizes us into the body of Christ.

Paul writes:

> For in one Spirit we were all baptized into one body—Jews or Greeks, slaves or free—and all were made to drink of one Spirit (1 Corinthians 12:13).

Spirit baptism is not exactly the same thing as water baptism. Spirit baptism takes place at the moment of regeneration. Water baptism takes place sometime later and is the outward and visible symbol, which points to the inward, spiritual reality of Spirit baptism. Water baptism is the decision of the believer to confess publicly what has happened to him or her. The human decision to request water baptism at the hands of the Christian community is dependent on, and a response to, the divine decision that was regeneration or new birth. God saves us; we respond in faith as those awakened from the sleep of death, newly enabled to respond to our Lord and our God.

Salvation is not synergy. That is, it is not the *cooperation* of humans with divine grace. This was the error of the medieval church that God used the Reformation to correct. Salvation involves human action as well as divine action; human action is not cooperation but a *response* elicited by divine grace.

4. The Holy Spirit seals us in Christ.

In Ephesians, Paul explains:

In him you also, when you heard the word of truth, the gospel of your salvation, and believed in him, were sealed with the promised Holy Spirit, who is the guarantee of our inheritance until we acquire possession of it, to the praise of his glory (Ephesians 1:13–14).

When you become a Christian, you become a joint heir with Jesus Christ of the riches of God. As a deposit on that inheritance, which you will one day receive in its fullness, you receive here and now the Holy Spirit. In other words, the presence of the Holy Spirit here and now in our lives is our guarantee that God will in fact do all that he has promised to do for us.

B. THE WORK OF THE HOLY SPIRIT IN THE LIVES OF BELIEVERS

In the lives of believers, the Holy Spirit does seven things:

1. The Holy Spirit indwells us.
Paul refers to this truth when he rebukes the Corinthians for their immoral lifestyles:

Do you not know that you are God's temple and that God's Spirit dwells in you? (1 Corinthians 3:16)

The Spirit of almighty God lives within you if you are a born again Christian. Is that not an incentive to holy living? Everywhere you go, you take God's Spirit with you. The Spirit indwells Christians continuously, even when we sin—that is why the Holy Spirit can be grieved. When we sin, we lose the filling of the Spirit, but we don't lose the Spirit. When we repent and ask God to fill us with his Spirit again, we can be filled with the Spirit again.

2. The Holy Spirit comforts us.
Jesus calls the Spirit the Comforter:

And I will ask the Father, and he will give you another Helper, to be with you forever (John 14:16).

The King James Version says "Comforter." In the English Standard Version the Greek word *parakletos* is rendered as "Helper." In the New International Version it is translated "Counselor." All these translations convey *aspects* of the meaning of this word. The Greek word literally means "one who comes alongside of." The Holy Spirit comes alongside us when we are discouraged or in crisis and comforts us. He is our strength and consolation in grief and our stronghold in times of trouble.

3. The Holy Spirit enables us to bear witness to Jesus Christ.

But you will receive power when the Holy Spirit has come upon you, and you will be my witnesses in Jerusalem and in all Judea and Samaria, and to the end of the earth (Acts 1:8).

Without the Spirit, we can do nothing. But in the power of the Spirit, we can preach the gospel with power and effect. It is really the Spirit of God working through us that makes Christian witness effective.

4. The Holy Spirit teaches us God's truth.
Jesus said:

When the Spirit of truth comes, he will guide you into all the truth (John 16:13).

The Spirit is the one who inspired the Holy Scriptures, and it is he who opens our eyes to the truth they contain. We need to rely on the Holy Spirit as we interpret the Scriptures. True scriptural interpretation is a prayer to the Holy Spirit for illumination.

5. The Holy Spirit guides us.
The Holy Spirit guides us as Christians, and he also guides the church as a whole. Paul writes:

For all who are led by the Spirit of God are sons of God (Romans 8:14).

Throughout the book of Acts, we see the Spirit's work of guiding the early church. The Spirit also guided the apostles as they wrote the writings that eventually became the New Testament, and the Holy Spirit guided the church as it recognized the canon of Scripture.

6. The Holy Spirit intercedes for us before the throne of God.

Likewise the Spirit helps us in our weakness. For we do not know what to pray for as we ought, but the Spirit himself intercedes for us with groanings too deep for words. And he who searches hearts knows what is the mind of the Spirit, because the Spirit intercedes for the saints according to the will of God (Romans 8:26–27).

Even when we are too depressed, too discouraged, too tired or too sick, the Holy Spirit prays for us. What a comfort to know this fact!

7. The Holy Spirit gives us assurance of salvation.
As Paul put it:

> For you did not receive the spirit of slavery to fall back into fear, but you have received the Spirit of adoption as sons, by whom we cry, "Abba! Father!" The Spirit himself bears witness with our spirit that we are children of God, and if children, then heirs—heirs of God and fellow heirs with Christ (Romans 8:15–17).

It is the Holy Spirit within us who gives us the final assurance of salvation. Our faith is not in ourselves or in our own experience, but in the Spirit of God who is alive and active within us.

II. I BELIEVE IN THE CHURCH

QUESTION 25: What does it mean to believe in "the holy catholic church, the communion of saints"?

The church is holy because all those who have put their trust in Jesus Christ have been made holy in him. The church is catholic because it includes all those who have put their trust in Jesus Christ whether they are on earth or in heaven. Each local church is a visible expression of the holy, catholic church.

All those who have put their trust in Jesus Christ have been made holy in him. The church is called "catholic" because it includes all those who have put their trust in Jesus Christ whether they are on earth or in heaven. Each local church is a visible expression of the holy, catholic church. Those who have put their trust in Christ have become part of his body, so the church and Christ are very closely identified with each other in the New Testament. This means that to believe in the church is to believe in Christ and that to believe in Christ is to believe in the church.

We need to expand on this answer by looking at the nature and mission of the church. First, let us consider the nature of the church by examining briefly the four "marks" of the church that are mentioned in the Niceno-Constantinopolitan Creed of A.D. 381.

A. THE NATURE OF THE CHURCH

1. The oneness or unity of the church

The true church is one. The true church consists of all those who are true Christians, in heaven and on earth, and the church is one body with Jesus Christ as the head. Paul's glorious vision of the church is given to us in Ephesians 4:1–16. Notice the stress here on the oneness of the church: one body, one Spirit, one Lord, one baptism, one God and Father. There are many offices and gifts in the church, but their function is to prepare God's people for service, so that as they become mature the image of Christ will become more and more apparent.

This passage also speaks of opposition to the unity of the church, and we can see with our own eyes that the church is sadly divided today. Jesus prayed, on the night before his crucifixion, that the church would be one:

> I do not ask for these only, but also for those who will believe in me through their word, that they may all be one, just as you, Father, are in me, and I in you, that they also may be in us, so that the world may believe that you have sent me (John 17:20–21).

Here we see the deepest meaning of the unity of the church. In loving and serving one another as Paul describes in Ephesians 4, we bear a witness to the unity of Jesus with the Father. The triune God is faintly but discernibly reflected in our life together.

Obviously, Satan does not want the oneness of the church to be visible, so he does all he can to stir up dissension, major on the minors and divide Christians from one another. Yet Jesus prayed for us. And the Holy Spirit prays for us now. God's will cannot ultimately be frustrated.

2. The holiness of the church

The true Church is holy. Now the church's holiness, it must be said right away, is not something that the church possesses in and of itself. The church is made up of sinners, after all. But the church is still holy. The most amazing sentence in Paul's first letter to the Corinthians comes in the second verse where he calls the Corinthian Christians holy:

> To the church of God that is in Corinth, to those sanctified in Christ Jesus, called to be saints together with all those who in every place call upon the name of our Lord Jesus Christ, both their Lord and ours (1 Corinthians 1:2).

The Corinthian church was torn apart by divisions, had all sorts of moral problems, were taking each other to court, and so on. But Paul refers to them as sanctified, which means "made holy." Why did he do so?

All those who have trusted Christ for salvation have been sanctified by their Spirit baptism into the body of Christ, and God looks upon them as pure and holy. This is sometimes called *positional sanctification*. It depends on our position or standing as those who belong to Christ. This is what Paul means by "those sanctified in Christ Jesus." But Paul also speaks of them as being "called to be holy," which hints at our calling to be made holy in our actual deeds, thoughts and motives as we live the Christian life. The church is already holy in one sense, but it is called to *become* holy in another sense. We have a new standing or position before God as forgiven people; now the goal of the Christian life is to live up to our new position.

But, of course, the church sins. The difference between the church and the world, however, is just this: The church knows that it is sinning and continuously repents. The church is not a museum for perfect specimens of Christianity, but a hospital for wounded sinners who know they are saints, but have not yet become what they are destined to be.

Many people look around at the divisions in the church, the scandals in the church and the weakness of the church in the face of the attacks of the enemy and wonder why the church seems so unholy. But we need to think of the difference between an army in peacetime and an army in the midst of war. In peacetime, everything is organized, clean and shiny. There are parades, orderly procedures, a clear chain of command and an atmosphere of strength and confidence. But in the midst of war, there are casualties, gaps in the ranks, confusion, a lack of clear communication and ineffectiveness. Battle breeds confusion and disorganization. There may be units operating in isolation from central command; some are behind enemy lines. Some have been captured by the enemy and the generals are often in the dark about what is actually going on. We live in a time of war, and if the church is an army, she is an army under siege and in disarray. Divisions, confusion and gaps are just what we should expect. Over there a brigade is surrendering to superior enemy forces; over here a platoon is decimated by casualties. But in other places, advances are being made and victories are being won. From our local situation it is not possible to see the big picture as God does, and we have to take it on faith that the Lord is ultimately going to win the war.

The key difference between the church and the world is that the church knows the truth about good and evil and can speak that truth because those of us in the church are sinners saved by grace. The good thing about being forgiven is that we can be honest about our faults. We do not need to be perfect in our moral lives—for the sin natures we still have will not let us be perfect in this life anyway. But we do have to act like we are really forgiven. The main way we do that is by forgiving one another just as God has forgiven us.

3. The catholicity of the church

The true church is catholic or universal. The word "catholic" simply means "universal" and the opposite of "catholic" is "sectarian" or "heretical off-shoot." The Jehovah's Witnesses and the Mormons are not catholic; they are heretical offshoots from the church. They are not Christian.

Some people ask why we say the Creed with the word "catholic" in it. Of course, their concern is that they don't want to endorse the Roman Catholic Church. Well, the catholic church is much bigger than the organization that recognizes the pope in Rome as the head of the church. The one, holy, catholic and apostolic church is not one denomination; it is not the Roman Catholic Church.

There is no doubt that we should want to be part of the true church, and the true church is catholic in the sense that it is not a sectarian, divisive, heretical offshoot from the main trunk of Christianity. The true church is catholic. Paul expresses the catholicity of the church when he says:

> For this reason I bow my knees before the Father, from whom every family in heaven and on earth is named (Ephesians 3:14–15).

The church is the whole family in heaven and earth—the whole people of God.

But as with the marks of unity and holiness, the catholicity of the church is ultimately an eschatological concept. We do not yet see the catholicity of the church in history, and we never will until we first see the unity of the church. But we walk by faith and not by sight, and we believe in the catholicity of the church.

4. The apostolicity of the church

The true church is apostolic. By apostolic we mean built on the foundation of the New Testament apostles, who were the appointed witnesses to the life, death, resurrection and ascension of the Lord Jesus. There are two main definitions of apostolicity. One is called *apostolic succession*, and it is stressed by Roman Catholics, Eastern Orthodox and Anglicans, who claim that their bishops or pastors are ordained in a historical sequence of ordinations going all the way back to the apostles who were with Jesus. The other definition of apostolic succession is *"conformity to the apostolic writings of the New Testament."* As Baptists, we are striving to be biblical churches.

The second definition of apostolicity is by far the most important. So-called apostolic succession cannot substitute for being biblical. Of course, in a general sense, there has to be a historical continuity between the apostles and us or else there would not be any historical continuity between Jesus and us. But mere institutional unity can never replace teaching what the apostles taught, preaching the gospel as it is defined in the New Testament and letting the Holy Scriptures be our authoritative rule of faith and practice.

In sum: The true church is one, holy, catholic and apostolic. We believe in the church even though the true beauty and perfection of the church has not yet been revealed. The church in history is rent by division, troubled by heresies, compromised in sin and attacked by the devil; yet the church exists and shall overcome. We look forward to the day when the church will be the beautiful bride of Christ and when her true nature will be revealed for all to see. We believe in the church as an article of faith.

B. THE MISSION OF THE CHURCH

In Acts 1:8, we have a succinct statement of the mission of the church by our Lord Jesus Christ himself:

> But you will receive power when the Holy Spirit has come upon you, and you will be my witnesses in Jerusalem and in all Judea and Samaria, and to the end of the earth (Acts 1:8).

The primary mission of the church is to be witnesses to Jesus Christ and in order to carry out this mission, the empowering of the Holy Spirit is essential. In Acts 2:42–47, we see a snapshot of the Spirit-filled, early church:

> And they devoted themselves to the apostles' teaching and the fellow-ship, to the breaking of bread and the prayers. And awe came upon every soul, and many wonders and signs were being done through the apostles. And all who believed were together and had all things in common. And they were selling their possessions and belongings and distributing the proceeds to all, as any had need. And day by day, attending the temple together and breaking bread in their homes, they received their food with glad and generous hearts, praising God and having favor with all the people. And the Lord added to their number day by day those who were being saved.

1. They devoted themselves to the apostles' teaching.
This is the fundamental requirement of any true church. The church is under the Word of God and the Word of God comes to us through the apostles. There are at least eight important implications of this truth for how we make use of the Bible in the church.

First, the Bible must be translated into the language of the people. Second, every believer should own, read, mark and meditate upon his own personal copy of the Bible. Third, the careful and reverent reading of the Word should be central in every worship service. Fourth, the centrepiece of every worship service should be the exposition of one or more passages of Scripture by a teacher, specially trained and set aside by the congregation for the purpose of studying the Scriptures full time. All other ministries in the church can be performed by part-time staff and lay people. This one, alone, requires special training and time. Churches need to free up their pastor for the ministry of the Word. Fifth, the Bible should inform and shape our music, our testimonies, our ethical deliberations and all aspects of our common life. Sixth, Christian education in the form of Bible centred instruction for all age groups in the church must be maintained. Every member should be studying the Bible individually, in a small group or class and in worship. No one of these methods substitutes for the lack of the other two. Seventh, in church business meetings, the highest authority must be the Bible. In discussion of what to do as a congregation, such as how to spend money or setting congregational priorities, everyone should recognize that our goal is to make our congregational life conform to the apostolic teaching of Scripture. This is the basis for debate and deliberation. Eighth, in our personal lives, the Bible must be our highest authority. We should expect to hear God speak to us through the Bible about our priorities, our vocations, our shortcomings, our life crises and our relationships. These things are part and parcel of what it means to devote ourselves to the apostles' teaching.

2. They worshipped together.
We read that they broke bread together (v. 42), they prayed (v. 42), they met together regularly in the temple courts and private homes (v. 46) and they praised God (v. 43). Worship involves at least five essential elements. First, it must be corporate—meeting together is a necessity. Second, the heart of worship is prayer—the church addresses God, and as we participate in this speaking, we as individuals learn how to talk to God for ourselves. Third, praise is an essential aspect of worship—we do this primarily through singing psalms, hymns and spiritual songs, as Paul puts it in Ephesians 5:19. Fourth, the Lord's Supper should be central to our worship service. For most of us in the believers' church tradition, the Lord's Supper or Eucharist is much too peripheral. It needs to be more central. Fifth, baptism is not mentioned here, but it is obviously part of the worship of the church and is mentioned earlier in this chapter. Worship involves the whole church coming together to acknowledge God as Lord and to make it clear that we belong to each other because we belong to God.

3. They were a fellowship of sharing.
We read they devoted themselves to fellowship (v. 42) and that members of the church sold possessions in order to "give to anyone as he had need" (v. 45).

We also read that they broke bread together in their homes and "ate together with glad and sincere hearts" (v. 46). Fellowship takes many forms in the church. We can note four of the most important, all of which can be observed in this passage. First, fellowship involves sharing that goes beyond the superficial—it involves really getting to know one another. Second, fellowship in large groups, therefore, must be supplemented by fellowship in small groups. The early Christians worshipped in the temple courts and also in private homes. We need to have small groups where we can really become transparent with one another and become accountable to one another. Third, economic sharing is foundational to fellowship. We need to care for one another in practical, down-to-earth ways, especially in times of crisis like death, sickness, job loss, persecution, depression, marital difficulties, and so on. Fourth, as we serve one another in Christ, we experience the ministry of the Spirit among us and we are knitted together in Christ.

4. As a result, the church grew by conversions.
The Lord added daily to their number those who were being saved (v. 47). It is interesting that evangelism seems here to be a by-product of body life, rather than a specific program or activity. It is clear that the life of the early church described here was a public life. The church was visible in Jerusalem and unbelievers could see it. People were attracted to the gospel when they saw it in action, and the same is true today. A healthy church will attract converts with minimal organized effort, but an unhealthy church will not attract converts no matter what.

III. I BELIEVE IN THE FORGIVENESS OF SINS

QUESTION 26: What does it mean to believe in "the forgiveness of sins"?

It means that we put our complete trust in the atoning death of Jesus Christ as our only hope for the forgiveness of our sins (Ephesians 1:7).

We are to put our complete trust in the atoning death of Jesus Christ as our only hope for the forgiveness of our sins. As Paul puts it in Ephesians: "In him we have redemption through his blood, the forgiveness of our trespasses, according to the riches of his grace" (Ephesians 1:7). The Holy Spirit is at work creating a people who are united in their conviction that the blood of Christ is the hope of the world.

We have already spoken of how the church is the community of those whose sins are forgiven and how this makes the church the church. The church is full of sinners just like the world, but the sinners in the church *know* they are sinners and also know that they are forgiven by the grace of God on the basis of Christ's atoning work on the cross. Our faith centres on Jesus Christ and the cross. When the cross is no longer central to a church, it has become a dead, heretical, mockery of a true church. Those who are in the church are those who know they are sinners, know that Christ has died for their sins and know they have forgiveness through his blood.

IV. I BELIEVE IN THE RESURRECTION OF THE BODY AND THE LIFE EVERLASTING

As Christians, we are not as those who are without hope. We live our lives in the light of the Christian hope of eternity.

> **QUESTION 27:** What does it mean to believe in "the resurrection of the body and the life everlasting"?
>
> ---
>
> It means to believe that on the day of judgement our bodies will be raised incorruptible and reunited with our souls so that in the new heavens and new earth we will live in glorified, resurrected bodies forever (Revelation 20:11–15; 21–22).

We believe in the resurrection of the *whole person*—body and soul—by the power of God.

The church has always rejected Gnosticism, a heretical set of doctrines that denigrates the body and views salvation as escaping this world, which is written off as lost and totally evil. Instead of believing that the creation is being redeemed and renewed by God, the Gnostics believe that creation cannot be redeemed because there is nothing good about it. The reason they believe this is because they have a *dualistic worldview* in which spirit is inherently good and matter is inherently evil. This is very different from Christianity in which *both* matter and spirit can be both good and evil. There are fallen as well as unfallen angels. The physical world was adversely affected by man's fall into sin, but the promise of Scripture is that the evil effects of the Fall (Genesis 3:14–19) will be undone and reversed by redemption (Isaiah 11:6–9). We look forward to the new heavens and new earth, but we do not look forward to a disembodied, purely spiritual existence in heaven. The fact that we look forward to the resurrection of our bodies means that we honour our bodies as temples of the Holy Spirit here and now. It means that we care about sexual morality and we care about acting with integrity with regard to our bodies.

CONCLUSION

The third article of the creed is a confession of our faith in the person and work of the Holy Spirit. Despite all appearances to the contrary, God is still sovereign, and he is at work in the world by his Spirit. The Spirit is applying the redemption accomplished by Christ's once for all sacrifice on the cross to individual believers, building them up into the body of Christ, the church, and is guiding history to its long-awaited consummation. One day, every knee will bow and every tongue will confess that Jesus Christ is Lord and that day will be a day of judgement. Christians can look forward to that day as one of vindication, as we are declared, "Not guilty!" because of the blood of Christ. We will also experience the resurrection of the body and life everlasting. This is what Christians believe.

Questions for reflection

1. Explain which mistakes concerning the doctrine of the Holy Spirit the following groups typically make: Roman Catholics, liberal Protestants, Pentecostals/charismatics and evangelicals. How can we have a balanced view of the Holy Spirit?

2. What are the four works of the Holy Spirit in salvation?

3. What are the seven works of the Holy Spirit in the life of believers?

4. How does the analogy of an army at war help us understand the weaknesses and divisions of the church in the contemporary world?

5. What are the two views of apostolic succession, and which one do evangelical Protestants hold?

6. If there is sin in the church as well as in the world, what is the difference between the church and the world?

8

What is baptism?

PART III
Baptism–Christian conversion
QUESTIONS 28–35

"Baptism is a sign of our conversion to Christ."

INTRODUCTION

At this point, we come to a hinge point in the catechism. We began by looking at what God requires of us. Jesus tells us that we are expected to love God with all our heart and soul and mind and our neighbour as ourselves. But we do not do that perfectly, and we cannot do that perfectly. Hence our dilemma as helpless lost sinners under divine judgement. Then we learned that there is hope if we believe the gospel, and we explored the Apostles' Creed to understand what the gospel teaches. Now, we come, in Part III of the catechism, to what it means to be converted.

QUESTION 28: If you believe that you are a miserable sinner who has failed to love God and neighbour as you ought and you believe that all is contained in the Apostles' Creed, how do you actually become a Christian?

The Word of God promises that "if you confess with your mouth that Jesus is Lord and believe in your heart that God raised him from the dead, you will be saved" (Romans 10:9).

QUESTION 29: What does it mean to "confess with your mouth that Jesus is Lord"?

The apostle Peter tells us the answer to this question in Acts 2 when he says, "Repent and be baptized every one of you in the name of Jesus Christ for the forgiveness of your sins, and you will receive the gift of the Holy Spirit" (Acts 2:38).

In the answer to Question 28, we learn that the Word of God says that one must: (i) confess with one's mouth that Jesus is Lord, and (ii) believe in one's heart that God has raised him from the dead. We must *confess* outwardly and *believe* inwardly.

Then, Question 29 refers us to the words of Peter in his sermon on the Day of Pentecost in Act 2:38. We are to believe in our hearts, confess with our mouths, repent of our sins and be baptized. This is the model of Christian conversion in Scripture. We are assured that when we do this we will receive the gift of the Holy Spirit.

As evangelical Christians, we believe that every person must come to the place of being born again. The New Testament way of showing this has occurred is that after repenting of our sins we show our faith in Jesus Christ by following him in the waters of baptism as a public testimony to our faith in him (John 3:1–6).

QUESTION 30: What is baptism?

Baptism is one of the two ordinances or sacraments of the church, which we perform in obedience to the command of our Lord Jesus Christ. To be baptized is to be immersed in water by a minister of a

Christian church in a public worship service on the basis of your
personal and verbal confession of faith in Jesus Christ.

Baptism is done, according to our Lord's explicit instructions in Matthew
28:18–20 in the three-fold name of the Father, the Son and the Holy Spirit.

QUESTION 31: Who should be baptized?

Only those who have first, reached the age of accountability; second,
repented of their sin; and, third, trusted Christ for salvation, are the
proper subjects of baptism.

What is the age of accountability? It is simply the age when a person becomes personally aware that he or she is a sinner and guilty before a holy
God. Why are infants not candidates for baptism? They cannot be baptized
because they cannot believe the gospel and repent of their sins. Baptism as
a ritual is of no value to anyone in and of itself, and the church does not
possess the power to confer grace on someone if the Holy Spirit is not
working in that person's heart to produce faith. Baptism loses its meaning
if it is reduced to a mindless ritual unrelated to faith and repentance and
comes to resemble magic more than a Christian sacrament of new birth.[1]

Baptism is a sign of something else—regeneration or new birth—and
cannot be separated from that of which it is a sign. The word "sign" is a
way of stressing the *sacramental nature* of baptism. In Christian theology, a
sacrament is a sign—a visible enactment of an inward and spiritual reality.
A sign (baptism) differs from the thing signified (regenerating grace) but it
points to and stands for it. There is a close relationship between them but
the two are not identical.

Some Protestants, in an over-reaction against the Roman Catholic
emphasis on the potency of the ritual in and of itself, go so far as to deny
the sacramental nature of baptism altogether. However, a true sacramental
theology holds together the necessity of faith and the connection of the
outward ritual to the spiritual reality of which it is a sign. To take the

---

[1] Roman Catholics believe in baptismal regeneration, that is, that babies are regenerated by baptism.
Most Reformed Protestants who practice infant baptism do not believe this. Instead, they would
see baptism as a sign of incorporation into the covenant community but not necessarily a guarantee
of regeneration. As Baptists, however, we believe that personal repentance and faith should be
linked as closely as possible with baptism, and that this is best done in believers' baptism.

non-sacramental approach to an even further extreme would be to refuse to baptize altogether, which the Salvation Army does. Our Lord commanded baptism—therefore it is an ordinance—and the New Testament teaches its true meaning. Believer's baptism is an outward sign of the inner reality of regeneration and conversion.

But if it is not magic or a mindless ritual unrelated to what is going on in the heart of the one being baptized, what exactly is the *meaning* of baptism according to the New Testament? We can organize biblical teaching on baptism under five headings.

I. BAPTISM AS A SIGN OF THE NEW COVENANT

All four Gospels describe the ministry of John the Baptist—he is the hinge between the Testaments. He was the last of the Old Testament prophets and the first New Testament apostle. He was the first to point to Jesus and say, "Behold, the Lamb of God, who takes away the sin of the world!" (John 1:29). It is important to note that John's message was one of purification in preparation for the coming of the Messiah (Matthew 3:2), and his baptism, therefore, was a baptism of repentance (Matthew 3:11).

The Old Testament (Old Covenant) was mainly, though not exclusively, focused on external behaviour because that is all that law can really address. One cannot command someone to have a change of heart; one can barely hope to command someone to do or refrain from doing certain things. For this reason, the Old Testament law only had the power to condemn. It was able to show us how far short of God's standards we fall. It was not able to produce a new heart of love and obedience toward God. But the Old Testament prophets, correctly diagnosing the real problem, prophesied about the coming day when God would make a New Covenant with his people, one that would be written on the heart. Jeremiah wrote:

> Behold, the days are coming, declares the LORD, when I will make a new covenant with the house of Israel and the house of Judah, not like the covenant that I made with their fathers on the day when I took them by the hand to bring them out of the land of Egypt, my covenant that they broke, though I was their husband, declares the LORD. For this is the covenant that I will make with the house of Israel after those days, declares the LORD: I will put my law within them, and I will write it on their hearts. And I will be their God, and they shall be my people (Jeremiah 31:31–33).

The Old Covenant was not bad, just *insufficient* for a fallen people. What they needed was not just *clarification* of what God's will really was, but *power* to obey it. This power to obey can only come from a transformation of the human heart and comes about only by the Spirit of God indwelling the believer and producing fruit.

Baptism is a sign of this New Covenant and contrasts with circumcision, the sign of the Old Covenant. It is a mistake to think of baptism as just a new circumcision; it is crucial that we see how the signs are different and reflect the difference between the two covenants spoken of by Jeremiah.

In Ephesians, Paul addressed the Gentiles, who are "called 'the uncircumcision' by what is called the circumcision, which is made in the flesh by hands," that is, the Jews (Ephesians 2:11). Here we have a reference to the external rite of circumcision symbolizing the obligation to keep the entire law of Moses. Paul could speak disparagingly about this circumcision, as in Galatians where he writes, "For in Christ Jesus neither circumcision nor uncircumcision counts for anything, but only faith working through love" (Galatians 5:6). But he also could speak of circumcision having a positive significance. For example, he writes of Abraham:

He received the sign of circumcision as a seal of the righteousness that he had by faith while he was still uncircumcised. The purpose was to make him the father of all who believe without being circumcised, so that righteousness would be counted to them as well (Romans 4:11).

Circumcision either was neutral and unimportant or highly significant to Paul depending on whether it was understood to be a sign of faith or of legalism. Christian baptism is to be contrasted with circumcision understood as legalism and ritualism, but is in continuity with circumcision understood as the sign of faith in God's promises.

Baptism is a sign of faith—this is its whole significance. Apart from faith it is of no more significance than circumcision. Baptism is a sign of the fulfilment of the promise of the New Covenant. In the New Covenant, baptism is a sign of the fulfilment of the promise: "And the LORD your God will circumcise your heart" (Deuteronomy 30:6). As Paul put it: "For no one is a Jew who is merely one outwardly, nor is circumcision outward and physical. But a Jew is one inwardly, and circumcision is a matter of the heart, by the *Spirit*, not by the *letter*" (Romans 2:28–29).

II. BAPTISM AS A SIGN OF SALVATION

Baptism is not only a sign of the New Covenant, it is a sign of salvation. Precisely because it is a sign of faith, it is a reminder that we cannot be saved by keeping the law. Paul quotes Leviticus 18:5: "the person who does the commandments shall live by them" (Romans 10:5). But who does this? In Romans 1 to 3 Paul explains that no one does this, no one keeps the commandments. Paul summarizes: "For by works of the law no human being will be justified in his sight, since through the law comes knowledge of sin" (Romans 3:20).

But we are not to despair, because Christ has done for us what we could never do for ourselves, in both his active and passive obedience. He lived a perfect life and overcame the temptation to sin (Matthew 4:1–11), and then he gave his life on the cross to atone for our sins and make it possible for us to be forgiven and reconciled to God by faith in Christ's saving death and resurrection. Our proper response to the gospel is not to ignore what Christ has done and try to save ourselves by keeping the law (which is impossible to do), but rather to believe the good news, repent of our sins and put our faith in Jesus Christ. When we believe in our hearts, confess with our mouths and repent of our sins, we are ready to be baptized as a sign of salvation.

Now we are in a position to appreciate the importance of the next two questions and answers.

QUESTION 32: What does it mean to call baptism a "sacrament"?

A sacrament is an outward and visible sign of an inward, spiritual reality. In baptism, the outward sign is water (Acts 2:38) and the spiritual reality is the new birth or being "born again," as our Lord explained to Nicodemus (John 3:3–5). Thus, water baptism is a visible and outward sign of an inward and spiritual reality. When the Holy Spirit regenerates us, we repent and believe and, water baptism follows as a testimony to this spiritual reality (Acts 10:47).

As human beings, we participate in both the physical and the spiritual worlds—we are made up of bodies (physical) and souls (spiritual). So it is fitting that an outward, physical thing (immersion in water in the name of the Father, the Son and the Holy Spirit) should be the sign of an inward, spiritual thing (regeneration or new birth). We should not play one off against the other as if only the spiritual is important. Both are important; baptism is an important part of Christian discipleship.

QUESTION 33: Can grace be imparted through a sacrament apart from personal faith on the part of the recipient?

No, God does not choose to impart grace except through personal

> faith on the part of the recipient. Water baptism apart from personal
> faith is useless.

Baptism as a ritual, apart from faith, is useless. However, baptism as an outward sign of inner faith is a sign of our salvation.

III. BAPTISM AS A SIGN OF THE HOLY SPIRIT

Baptism is not only a sign of the New Covenant and of our salvation, it is also a sign of the Holy Spirit. When we are regenerated, we are baptized in the Holy Spirit. John hinted at this when he said that while he baptized with water, Jesus would baptize with the Holy Spirit (Mark 1:8).

What is the relationship between water baptism and Spirit baptism? This is a difficult question that has caused many theologians to trip and fall. The problem is that there *is* a relationship between them, but expressing that relationship too strongly leads to heresy. Since the sixteenth century, most Protestants have rejected as heretical and unbiblical the Roman Catholic doctrine of baptismal regeneration because that doctrine has been interpreted as regeneration through the ritual of water baptism *apart from faith*. The fact is, Spirit baptism, regeneration and faith are very closely linked and water baptism is meant to be a sign of all of them. One can see how easy it is to go wrong on this issue.

Sometimes when people refer to baptism, they mean water baptism only, sometimes they mean Spirit baptism only and sometimes they mean both. It would help if we never used the word baptism without one or both qualifiers according to the meaning in that situation. For example, someone might ask, "Can I be saved without being baptized?" We might jump to the conclusion that the question is referring to *water* baptism alone, in which case the answer is "Yes," especially in certain situations, such as a death-bed conversion. But if one means *Spirit* baptism, then it is like asking, "Can I be saved without being born again?" If that is the meaning, then the answer is "No, it is impossible except perhaps in the case of infants who die before the age of accountability." Every genuine Christian has been baptized in the Spirit. As Paul writes, "Anyone who does not have the Spirit of Christ does not belong to him" (Romans 8:9). So, it is important to be precise in what one is saying and not saying.

There also may be misunderstandings between Roman Catholic and Protestant theologians over what is meant by baptismal regeneration. Protestants may assume only water baptism is in view, while Roman Catholics may assume both water and Spirit baptism are in view. What we should say categorically is *we do not believe that a sacrament can save anyone apart from faith produced in one's heart by the Spirit of God.* We also have to reckon with the fact that the Spirit works through baptism, which is his appointed sign of his presence. John Calvin, the great sixteenth-century Protestant Reformer, wrote:

> We do not deny that God himself is present in his institution by the very-present power of his Spirit. Nevertheless...we declare that the inner grace of the Spirit, as distinct from the outward ministry, ought to be considered & pondered separately.... They [the sacraments] do not bestow any grace of themselves, but announce and tell us...those things given by the divine bounty.... The sacraments have the same office as the Word of God: to offer and set forth Christ to us"[2]

No one upheld the doctrine of justification by faith alone more strongly that Calvin, but he was not ready to say that the Holy Spirit does not work through baptism. As can be seen from this quotation, however, Calvin was careful to separate the Spirit's working from the ritual in and of itself.

We have seen that water baptism does not convey grace in and of itself and it is possible to be baptized and still remain a non-Christian. A question may arise at this point: If we are saved by the activity of the Holy Spirit in regenerating us inwardly, why is baptism necessary at all? Any answer to this question must start with the recognition that Jesus *commanded* baptism in the three-fold name for all those who believe in their hearts, confess with their mouths and repent of their sins. It is not an *option*, because it was ordained by Christ himself. The word "ordinance," which is often applied to baptism and the Lord's Supper, comes from the root of "to ordain" or command or order. Jesus ordained baptism for his people. So it is a command of the Lord, and those who submit themselves to Jesus as Lord will want to obey him.

But what if someone did not obey Jesus in this matter? Could that person be a saved but disobedient Christian? Do we not disobey in other ways without losing our salvation? At this point, we need to see that there is a kind of parallel between baptism as a response of discipleship to the lordship of Christ and good works as evidence of having been born again. Some people mistakenly think that Paul and James contradict one another on the relationship between faith and works. Paul says that we are saved by faith alone (Ephesians 2:8–9); James says that faith without works is dead (James 2:17). Each is emphasizing one side of the truth. Saving faith always

[2] John Calvin, *Institutes of the Christian Religion*, ed. John T. McNeill, trans Ford Lewis Battles (Philadelphia: The Westminster Press, 1960), 4.14.17, 1293.

issues forth in the fruit of the Spirit, and therefore good works will characterize the life of every person who had been born again by faith in Christ. It is not that the works cause the faith, but that the faith causes the works. It is not faith in works, but rather, faith that works. It is similar with baptism. Being baptized will not save anyone, but anyone who really is saved will want to follow Jesus Christ in the first work of Christian discipleship. If someone refuses to obey Jesus at this point, we are justified in wondering whether that person really is born again. Baptism is a sign of the presence and working of the Holy Spirit.

IV. BAPTISM AS A SIGN OF UNION WITH CHRIST

Baptism is not only a sign of the New Covenant, salvation and the Holy Spirit, it is also a sign of our union with Christ.

QUESTION 34: What does baptism signify?

The apostle Paul tells us that to go down under the water is to identify with Jesus Christ in his death and to come up from the water is to identify with Jesus Christ in his resurrection. Thus, baptism signifies our union with Christ through faith (Romans 6:1–5).

Union with Christ is the master image for salvation in the New Testament. It includes within itself many other separate aspects of salvation.

The "order of salvation" includes ten steps or aspects of salvation: election, calling, regeneration, conversion, justification, adoption, sanctification, perseverance, death and glorification. Election takes place in eternity past. Calling, regeneration, conversion, justification and adoption all take place at almost the same time, centred around that moment when we pass from death into life. Sanctification then goes on for the rest of our earthly lives and is progressive. At death we pass into the presence of Christ (2 Corinthians 5:8), and on the day of resurrection we receive our glorified bodies that we will have for eternity (1 Corinthians 15:35–44). If you ask at which point are we united with Christ, the answer must be that in all the various aspects of salvation, from regeneration to glorification. Even election and effectual calling look forward to, and are for the purpose of, our union with Christ. If we had to say what salvation is using only one phrase, we could hardly do better than "union with Christ."

The answer to question 34 references Romans 6. We must take a closer look at this important passage:

We were buried therefore with him by baptism into death, in order that, just as Christ was raised from the dead by the glory of the Father, we too might walk in newness of life. For if we have been united with him in a death like his, we shall certainly be united with him in a resurrection like his (Romans 6:4–5).

When the person goes down into the water, it is like being laid in a grave and being buried as the water closes over the person's head. This symbolizes our dying with Christ. When the person is brought up out of the water (the grave), it is like a resurrection to new life in Christ. This symbolizes the eternal life we have by virtue of being united with Christ. To be united with Christ in his death and resurrection is to have new life in him. We were dead in our sins before, and now we are dying to sin as we are progressively sanctified.

In the first five chapters of Romans, Paul was stressing that salvation is by faith alone. In chapter 6, he deals with the question of whether this emphasis on grace and faith means that we should be indifferent to sin and just go ahead and live in sin. He emphatically denies that we should live in sin that grace may abound (Romans 6:1–2) and then gives the illustration of baptism to show what is our true identity as Christians. If we really know who we are, we will not live in sin, because we will know that we have died to sin and have been raised to a new and holy life in Christ. A new power is at work in us—the power of the Holy Spirit! We are being renewed in our inner being and made progressively into the image and likeness of Jesus Christ. We have the motivation to resist temptation, and we have a new power to do so that we did not have before.

V. BAPTISM AS A SIGN OF CHRISTIAN UNITY

Baptism is not only a sign of the New Covenant, salvation, the Holy Spirit and union with Christ, it is also a sign of Christian unity.

> **QUESTION 35:** Does baptism signify anything else?
>
> Yes, by virtue of being united to Christ, we also become part of his body the church. This is why we believe that believers' baptism is the prerequisite for local church membership (1 Corinthians 12:12–13).

Since baptism is a sign of being part of the *universal church*, it should be closely linked to being part of the *visible, local church* as well. There should be no such thing as a person being baptized and not becoming a member of a local church at the same time. In fact, we should not baptize a person who requested baptism but was not willing to join the church at the same time because not to join a local church is to deny part of the meaning of baptism. Paul writes:

> For just as the body is one and has many members, and all the members of the body, though many, are one body, so it is with Christ. For in one Spirit we were all baptized into one body—Jews or Greeks, slaves or free—and all were made to drink of one Spirit (1 Corinthians 12:12–13).

CONCLUSION

Baptism is a sign of the New Covenant promised in the Old Testament and instituted by Jesus Christ. It is a sign of our salvation. It is a sign of the presence and power of the Holy Spirit. It is a sign of our union with Christ. It is a sign of Christian unity in the body of Christ, the church. Baptism is commanded by Christ for those who follow him as Lord. It is a powerful testimony to the grace of God and to the gospel preached by the church. It is a gift and a privilege for all those who have experienced the grace of God in their lives.

Questions for reflection

1. If someone were to ask you how to become a Christian, what would you say?

2. What is a sacrament?

3. Could a person refuse to be baptized and still be saved? Why or why not?

4. What are the ten elements of salvation within the master metaphor of "union with Christ"?

9

Do the Ten Commandments apply to us today?

PART IV
The Ten Commandments—Christian ethics
QUESTIONS 36–42

"The Ten Commandments clarify the natural law
and properly form conscience."

INTRODUCTION

People have been breaking the natural law since Cain murdered his brother Abel. But our society has *legalized* and *approved* of breaking the natural law, which is known to all rational human beings from nature. People in every society since the Fall have broken the natural law, and the rate of law-breaking varies widely between societies and in different periods of history. But any given society has to degenerate to an extreme state of lawlessness before it actually begins to legalize and publicly endorse the breaking of the natural law on a wide scale by giving social approval to murder and sexual perversion.

Think of two possible scenarios. In scenario one, we might imagine a tough neighbourhood in which unwary, late night pedestrians are occasionally mugged and beaten up. But imagine a scenario two in which things are much worse. What would we say about a neighbourhood in which people poured out of their apartments and houses to cheer on the muggers and shout obscenities at the victims? What if the police arrived only to shake hands with the criminals and congratulate them on leaving the victim as a bloody mess? What if someone called 911 and the ambulance refused to come, saying that the victim "had it coming" and they were too busy? In the first scenario, society has a problem with crime—a form of social deviance. In the second scenario, society itself is the problem—the whole of the society has become deviant. We live in a society in which the murder of unborn children is routine, in which impersonal, animalistic sex separated from personal commitment is regarded as normal and in which killing inconvenient people is legal. Western society has now reached a state of extreme degeneration in which natural law has being rejected, scorned and denied. We are in a nightmarish version of scenario two in which occasional lawless behaviour has morphed into institutionalized, anti-law attitudes.

Natural law says that murder, adultery and stealing are wrong; contemporary Western society says these things are sometimes wrong and sometimes right, depending on the consequences of doing them or not doing them. Sometimes the mask slips a bit and it is acknowledged that it is not even an ethic of consequences that is operative here, it is merely a matter of the will of the strong prevailing over the hapless weak.

Only in such a society, in which natural law is denied and mocked, would anyone think of asking if the Ten Commandments still apply to us. The problem is that society is intolerant of any form of law except that invented by those in power in society on the basis of their own imperious will to power. Law that comes from nature or the Creator is seen as a threat to human freedom and autonomy. We live in a lawless and law-hating age. So, naturally, all law is seen as bad. In this cultural context, we even hear voices within the church questioning the validity and applicability of law to Christians. The voice may be the voice of Christian leaders, but the thoughts come from the spirit of the age, which gives expression to the mind of hell.

We can see what God thinks of the spirit of anti-law that pervades modern society in the name that is given to the Antichrist by Paul. In 2 Thessalonians 2, Paul tells us the end cannot come until the "man of lawlessness" is revealed (v.3). Who is this "man of lawlessness"? He is one who exalts himself "proclaiming himself to be god" (v.4). According to Paul, the "mystery of lawlessness" is already at work in the world, but is being restrained. Once the one who is restraining the man of lawlessness is removed (Paul is not entirely clear about the identity of this restrainer), the man of lawlessness will be revealed (v.7) and history will come to a climax with Jesus killing him by the breath of his mouth (v.8). Paul explains that the power of the man of lawlessness comes from Satan (v.9). The identification of the Antichrist with "lawlessness" shows the extent to which the hatred of law is ultimately satanic.

We can contrast this attitude of extreme hatred of law with the attitude of the psalmist, who speaks for the people of God when he exclaims, "Blessed are those whose way is blameless, who walk in the law of the LORD!" (Psalm 119:1). In the Bible, the law is a *blessing* from God and a source of life, joy and peace. The hatred of law in our society ultimately stems from a hatred of God and a spirit of rebellion against God, which is expressed in rebellion against his law. In this chapter, we explore the relationship between the natural law, conscience and the revealed law seen in the Ten Commandments.

I. NATURAL LAW

QUESTION 36: Can we know what is right and wrong?

Yes, we know right from wrong by discerning natural law by the light of conscience (Romans 1:18–32).

Paul makes this point vigorously in Romans 1:18–32 as the basis of his condemnation of the Gentiles. All people from the beginning of history have discerned right and wrong by their own reason without the need for any divine revelation or command. When Cain killed Abel, he knew it was wrong. He did not need a parliament to meet and deliberate before passing a law prohibiting murder. He did not need to go to church and hear a sermon on how God detests envy and jealousy. He just knew. Likewise, when people today break the natural law, they know at some level of their beings that what they are doing is wrong.

In the first major section of Romans, that is Romans 1:18–3:19, Paul discusses the sinfulness of the Gentiles (1:18–32), of the Jews (2:1–3:8) and of all people (3:9–20). His conclusion is: "None is righteous, no not one" (3:10). We need to focus on the first chapter because there Paul addresses the question of how the entire Gentile world, which has not been given the special revelation provided to the Jews from Abraham on, could be under divine wrath. Paul does not beat around the bush. He opens the section with a word of judgement: "For the wrath of God is revealed from heaven against all ungodliness and unrighteousness of men" (1:18). The Gentiles are under judgement. Why? They have suppressed the natural law they clearly perceived because they wanted to rebel against God. Listen to what he says:

For the wrath of God is revealed from heaven against all ungodliness and unrighteousness of men, who by their unrighteousness suppress the truth. For what can be known about God is plain to them, because God has shown it to them. For his invisible attributes, namely, his eternal power and divine nature, have been clearly perceived, ever since the creation of the world, in the things that have been made. So they are without excuse (Romans 1:18–20).

The reason the Gentiles rob, murder and commit adultery is not that they didn't know any better. The reason is that they *did* know better and did these things *anyway*. That is why God holds them responsible and why they are under a sentence of death.

Paul goes on to chronicle the descent of societies into madness and self-destructive behaviour. In verses 21–23 he describes how their minds became darkened and "claiming to be wise, they became fools" worshipping dead idols and birds and animals instead of the Creator. In verses 24–28 he describes how such people began to engage in sexual perversions, like homosexuality, as in their behaviour they denied the reality of a created order and a Creator. In verses 29–31, the next step in their descent is to belch up a whole list of ugly sins and vices, including everything from gossip to foolishness to deceit. Finally, in verse 31, they hit rock bottom by reaching the point where they are so perverted, so confused, so recklessly rebellious that they actually begin to call good evil and evil good. They not only break the natural law but they give open approval to those who do so. They have descended to the level of scenario two described above.

II. CONSCIENCE

QUESTION 37: Why then do we sin by breaking the natural law and thus going against conscience?

We do so because we have inherited a corrupt nature from our first parents, Adam and Eve, who fell into sin and came under the curse (Genesis 3).

We are sinners because we were born sinners. This is the doctrine of original sin. Adam and Eve were the first human beings to sin, and the consequences of their sin reverberate through the centuries and affect us all. How so?

There are two effects of original sin on the descendants of Adam and Eve. First, we inherit a defective nature—a fallen nature that is inherently weak and susceptible to temptation. We are sinners. Second, we also inherit guilt because in addition to being guilty for committing *actual* acts of sin, we are guilty for *being* sinners. Our situation is grim, and we are unable to save ourselves. We do not just *happen* to sin; we sin by *nature* as well as by *choice*, and it is our nature that determines our choices. The answer to why we sin by breaking the natural law is that we do it because we are sinners; sinful actions are the inevitable fruit of a sinful nature. We go against our consciences because we are fallen creatures who are affected by sin in every part of our beings.

QUESTION 38: Is conscience infallible?

No, one's conscience can become seared through repeatedly going against it so that it no longer works properly (Romans 1:28).

The descent into madness described in Romans 1:18–32 explains how conscience ceases to work properly in sinful people. Even sinners who commit acts of sin may still have a functioning conscience. Each person is born with a conscience, and it does not simply disappear the moment we sin for the first time. We have to sin over and over again in order to dull the conscience to the point of rendering it silent. Conscience is not destroyed by a single act of sin, but it can be bludgeoned into submission by repeated vice, reinforced by an evil will. Even then, it actually disappears completely only in rare cases. We call such people sociopaths, and they seem so unusual we affix to them a label because they seem to have a mental disorder. The relationship between the mental disorder and vice is extremely complicated, but what we can say for sure is that conscience is not indestructible and is not an all or nothing proposition. Conscience is part of the image of God in men and women, but like all aspects of that image, it is marred by original sin. We all have a conscience, but some have a "tender" conscience while others have a conscience that has been dulled by repeated acts of sinful self-indulgence.

QUESTION 39: What happens when our conscience no longer works properly?

Three things result from being in such a dangerous spiritual condition: first, we no longer recognize the existence of God from his works; second, we can no longer perceive the natural law of God; and third, our conscience no longer accuses us of law-breaking when we sin.

These are sobering truths. This is where atheism comes from, and atheism leads to an inability to see the natural law as real and true. In extreme cases, the final outcome of such a condition is moral inversion, that is, calling good evil and evil good. In the long slide from unthankfulness to idolatry to sin to perversion to advocating evil in Romans 1:18–32, the bottom of the slope is not only being unable to discern what is true and good, but urging others to commit evil as if it were good (v.32). This condition is so dangerous because it leaves us not only in danger, but totally oblivious to that danger. Conscience is like nerves in our bodies that send pain signals to the brain when the body is being harmed so we know enough to take our hand off the hot stove before it is completely burned. A person who cannot sense pain is in a dangerous situation, and the person who cannot sense sin is likewise in grave peril.

In society today, we see the widespread appeal of a facile, intellectually shallow atheism. Why do people believe such rubbish? It is because they have suppressed the knowledge of God and become fools (Psalm 53:1). We also see a widespread denial of the plain facts of natural law that is all around us. People prefer superstitious nonsense to the obvious, rational truth, because the truth constitutes a limit on their lusts. Many people today actually believe that a man can become a woman just by deciding he wants to do so. They actually believe willpower can help you change your sex anytime you like. The same people also irrationally insist that no person with an attraction to people of the same sex can change that "orientation" by any means whatsoever and, therefore, it should be illegal to try to help such a person who wants to change through counselling. Logical consistency is one of the early casualties of lawlessness. Damage to our conscience goes hand in hand with damage to our powers of reason.

III. THE TEN COMMANDMENTS

QUESTION 40: What has God mercifully given to sinners in this dangerous spiritual conditon?

He has given to us the Ten Commandments, which are his moral law in his own words.

The Ten Commandments are the biblical summary of the moral law of God for those who can no longer see the natural law.

FOUR KINDS OF LAW

1. **ETERNAL LAW** – the laws by which God governs the universe, including scientific laws and moral laws and which exist in his mind and reflect his nature.

2. **NATURAL LAW** – this is the part of the eternal law that is imprinted on creation by God and which can be known by human reason.

3. **HUMAN LAW** – created by human governments; they are supposed to be based on the natural law but may deviate from it because of the sinfulness of human society.

4. **BIBLICAL LAW** – or revealed law, is the law found in Scripture given to clarify what is obscured by sin so that we can understand why we need divine grace.

Thomas Aquinas (1225–1274), the great medieval theologian, helpfully distinguished between four kinds of law: eternal law, natural law, human law and biblical law.[1] All law is ultimately derived from the mind of God and reflects the nature of God. None of these four kinds of law conflict with one another. The creation of man in the image of God with a rational soul makes it possible for man to discern God's law in nature except when sin interferes with the proper function of reason. The problem is, as we have seen from Romans 1, sin often prevents us from seeing the truth right in front of us. To put it bluntly: Sin makes us stupid.

This is why God has given us the Ten Commandments. It was an act of grace on God's part to do so. We need to be shocked out of our stupor and brought face to face with reality. This is why the psalmist praises the law of God so highly as, for example, in Psalm 119. John Calvin wrote:

> Now the law has power to exhort believers. This is not a power to bind their consciences with a curse, but one to shake off their sluggishness by repeatedly urging them, and to pinch them awake to their imperfection.[2]

---

[1] Thomas Aquinas, *Summa Theologica*, trans. Fathers of the English Dominican Province, 5 vol. (Notre Dame: Ava Maria Press, 1920), I, 2, Question 91, articles 2 and 4, 996-1001, and Question 93, articles 2, 4, 5, 1003-1008.

[2] Calvin, *Institutes*, 2.7.14, 362.

The image is apt; we need to be pinched awake if we are to experience the freedom of the children of God.

The Bible does not see freedom as the unrestricted ability to do whatever comes into one's mind at any given moment. Rather, the Bible sees freedom as the ability of the rational mind to discern the good and then have the will and passions be subject to the mind and to desire the good. Freedom is the ability to do the good, whereas the ability to choose either the good or evil is a defect. The choice to do evil is, in our experience, the result of the downward pull of the passions in defiance of our rational minds. This is called *slavery* in Scripture, not freedom. The revealed law of God is a tool the rational mind can use to force the stubborn passions into line, and even if we don't resist the temptation to sin, we are reminded that sin is, in fact, exactly what we are doing. The revealed law of God makes rationalizing our sin more difficult and thus threatens to puncture our smug attitude of selfishness. In Scripture, we find true freedom by obeying God's law and, in order to do that, we need divine empowerment by the Spirit of God.

QUESTION 41: Why did God give us the Ten Commandments?

He gave us his law for three reasons: first, as a mirror in which we can see the danger of our true spiritual condition and be motivated to repent; second, as a republication of the natural law, so that we can know the basic laws that make life in community possible; and third, as a spur to a life of holiness, as we strive to be holy as God is holy (Leviticus 19:2).

So, the law shows us our need to repent and be forgiven, it restrains wickedness and preserves human society, and it reveals God's will for holy living to Christians.

Some Christians may object, saying, "we are not under the law but under grace" (Romans 6:15), and there is a great truth in that statement, but also the potential for misunderstanding. We are no longer subject to the condemnation of the law, because we have been justified by the blood of Christ and now stand before God clothed in the righteousness of Christ. That is the sense in which the law no longer applies; we are no longer condemned by it. But to imagine that God has saved us from sin just so we can continue to wallow in that from which we have been saved would be preposterous. Christians are called to "walk by the Spirit, and you will not gratify the desires of the flesh" (Galatians 5:16). True Christian freedom is the ability to do the good and refrain from doing evil. The fruit of the Spirit is law-abiding freedom; it is "love, joy, peace, patience, kindness, goodness, faithfulness, gentleness, self-control; against such things there is no law" (Galatians 5:22–23). The desires of the sinful flesh, on the other hand (Galatians 5:19–21), break God's law and lead to death.

Christ is the "end" or "goal" (*telos*) of the law (Romans 10:4). This means that Christ is the goal toward which the law tends. To be in Christ, and to be filled with his Spirit, is to be able to fulfil the law in the sense of living the kind of life it was intended to produce. The Old Testament law was intended to bring us to Christ, because only Christ can bring us to a place where the law achieves its goal in our lives.

We can distinguish between three kinds of law in the Old Testament: the moral law (the heart of which is the Ten Commandments), the ceremonial law (the sacrificial system and the temple) and the civil law (the laws pertaining to Israel as a nation). Christ fulfils all three kinds of law. For those who are in Christ, the ceremonial and civil laws no longer apply—we have the reality to which they pointed all along. The moral law is also fulfilled in Christ because the fruit of the Spirit results in us keeping the law and taking it to a higher plane—where we fulfil its *intent* as well as its *letter*. In the Sermon on the Mount, Jesus deepened the meaning of the law when he said: "Do not think that I have come to abolish the Law or the Prophets; I have not come to abolish them but to fulfill them" (Matthew 5:17). The law was our schoolmaster or guardian to bring us to Christ, as Paul explains in Galatians 3:23–25. But once we get to Christ, we no longer need the law as such, because we have the One who is the source of the law in the first place. If we recall Thomas Aquinas' four kinds of law, we can say that the biblical law points us back to the eternal law in the mind of God and, since we have the mind of Christ (1 Corinthians 2:16), we have internalized the law. This is exactly what the prophet Jeremiah predicted was going to happen in the New Covenant: "I will put my law within them, and I will write it on their hearts" (Jeremiah 31:33).

CONCLUSION: GOSPEL AND LAW

The law of God is really a blessing, not a curse. It only seems like a curse to those who seek to be their own god, in rebellion against the one, true God of the Bible. It really becomes a curse to them because it condemns them, and God lets his wrath fall on them. But to those who worship God and seek to serve him, his law is sweetness and life itself. The reason why the law is so precious to those who have been set free from the slavery of sin is that it is our charter of freedom. In Exodus 20, the giving of the Ten Commandments is prefaced with this statement: "I am the LORD your God, who brought you out of the land of Egypt, out of the house of slavery"

(Exodus 20:2). Notice that God has already set Israel free from slavery in Egypt. They are not given the Ten Commandments as the requirements they must fulfil in order to be worthy to be set free by God. The gospel message is that *deliverance precedes obedience*. Having been set free is the prerequisite for being enabled to keep God's law. It is not a duty but a privilege; it is not a burden but a delight. It is as if God had said: "Now I have set you free; here is how you stay free: Do these things."

QUESTION 42: Should we regard the Ten Commandments as a burden or as a blessing?

We should regard them as a gift of God's grace to poor sinners who need to hear God's command, in order to know clearly the difference between right and wrong and the way of holiness.

The giving of the law is a divine act of grace and mercy. Hopefully, by this point, it is plain how true that is.

Questions for reflection

1. What are some examples of how modern Western society has institutionalized attitudes of hatred toward God's law?

2. What are some of the blessings the author of Psalm 119 sees as flowing from the law of God?

3. How would you answer a person who justifies his or her acts of sexual deviance by saying, "My conscience is clear, so it cannot be wrong for me"?

4. Many people today view freedom as the ability to do whatever they want. How is the biblical idea of freedom defined in this chapter?

10

How do we obey the Ten Commandments today?

PART IV
The Ten Commandments—Christian ethics
QUESTIONS 43–55

"The Ten Commandments reveal the shape
of a holy, Christian life."

INTRODUCTION

In the previous chapter we saw that the Ten Commandments were given to us by God for our own good, and we should regard them as a blessing to be embraced joyfully. The moral law of God reflects the eternal law of God and never goes out of date. Since our minds are clouded by sin, the republication of the natural law in the form of the Ten Commandments in Scripture is a gift of God's grace to us, helping us to clearly discern the will of God for our lives. The Ten Commandments reveal to us the shape of the holy life to which all genuine Christians aspire. The purpose of this chapter is to examine the meaning of the commandments one at a time, so that we can understand what it means to obey the Ten Commandments today. We begin by looking at the structure of the Ten Commandments.

I. THE STRUCTURE OF THE TEN COMMANDMENTS

QUESTION 43: How do the Ten Commandments relate to the Great Commandment of Jesus?

The Great Commandment of our Lord Jesus Christ (Matthew 22:37–30) is a summary of the Ten Commandments (Exodus 20:1–17; Deuteronomy 5:1–21).

QUESTION 44: How are the Ten Commandments structured?

They are divided into two tablets: the first four contain our duty to God, and the last six contain our duty to our neighbour.

The Great Commandment of Jesus summarizes and mirrors the structure of the Ten Commandments by focusing on the love of God and the love of neighbour.

When Moses came down from Mount Sinai, he was carrying two stone tablets, which had been written on by God himself (Exodus 32:15–16). The Ten Commandments were thus symbolically declared to originate not in Moses as a human lawgiver, but in God as the ultimate Lawgiver. The Ten Commandments are divine law.

Our duty to God is contained on the first tablet and our duty to our neighbour is on the second. They constitute a complete expression of God's will for man. John Calvin notes that the further detail (Exodus 32:15) that they "were written on both sides" indicates the *completeness* of the law. All that God wanted us to know is here—albeit in highly compressed form—and it is, therefore, a worthwhile and legitimate endeavour to study each of the commandments carefully in order to draw out from them the implications they have for our lives. Although there are many other detailed applications of the moral law and specific requirements given in the rest of the Pentateuch, they are all to be regarded as elaborations of the Ten Commandments in one way or another. The beating heart of the entire law of God is seen in these Ten Commandments.

When Jesus was asked what is the greatest commandment, he summed up the Ten Commandments by saying the greatest commandment is to "love the Lord your God with all your heart and with all your soul and with all your mind." Then he added that a second is like it: "You shall love your neighbor as yourself" (Matthew 22:37–39). Everything else in the law flows from these two central principles.

One thing we should note, however, is the significance of the order: our duty to God precedes our duty to one another. First, we must get right with God, and only then can human relationships have any hope of being just. Our obedience to God is the prerequisite and foundation of our love for our fellow human beings and must take precedence. As Peter said to the Jewish authorities in Jerusalem when they commanded him to stop preaching about Jesus, "We must obey God rather than men" (Acts 5:29). Our love for neighbour grows out of our love for God as our highest priority. These are not in conflict. In fact, our love for God enables and necessitates love for our neighbour. But we love God, as Augustine frequently put it, for his own sake and our fellow man for the sake of God.[1]

If we try to invert the order, we will run into trouble. We cannot love God by loving the neighbour more than God, and we cannot make loving the neighbour our highest priority, assuming that by doing so we will be loving God in the process. No, we must love God first and foremost and then love God in the neighbour in such a way that even in loving the neighbour we are still, in actuality, loving God. To truly love God will necessarily and inevitably result in love of neighbour, but to try to love the neighbour in a godless way will only lead to making an idol out of human beings.

II. THE MEANING OF THE TEN COMMANDMENTS

As we approach the actual commandments, it is important to have them committed to memory. To review, Question 45 asks us to recite them:

QUESTION 45: What are the Ten Commandments?

And God spoke all these words, saying, "I am the LORD your God, who brought you out of the land of Egypt, out of the house of slavery."

1. You shall have no other gods before me.
2. You shall not make for yourself a carved image, or any likeness of anything that is in heaven above, or that is in the earth beneath, or that is in the water under the earth. You shall not bow down to them or serve them, for I the LORD your God am a jealous God, visiting the iniquity of the fathers on the children to the third

---

[1] Augustine, *On Christian Doctrine*, 1, 23, 22.

and the fourth generation of those who hate me, but showing steadfast love to thousands of those who love me and keep my commandments.

3. You shall not take the name of the LORD your God in vain, for the LORD will not hold him guiltless who takes his name in vain.

4. Remember the Sabbath day, to keep it holy. Six days you shall labor, and do all your work, but the seventh day is a Sabbath to the LORD your God. On it you shall not do any work, you, or your son, or your daughter, your male servant, or your female servant, or your livestock, or the sojourner who is within your gates. For in six days the LORD made heaven and earth, the sea, and all that is in them, and rested on the seventh day. Therefore the LORD blessed the Sabbath day and made it holy.

5. Honor your father and your mother, that your days may be long in the land that the LORD your God is giving you.

6. You shall not murder.

7. You shall not commit adultery.

8. You shall not steal.

9. You shall not bear false witness against your neighbor.

10. You shall not covet your neighbor's house; you shall not covet your neighbor's wife, or his male servant, or his female servant, or his ox, or his donkey, or anything that is your neighbor's.
(Exodus 20:1–17)

Note how the recitation of the Ten Commandments given in this answer begins with the prologue in verse 1 rather than with the actual first commandment in verse 3. Here we see, as we noted in the last chapter, the gospel that precedes the law. The reference is to God's mighty act of deliverance in the Exodus from Egypt. First God saves us, and then we serve him. It cannot be the other way around, because until we are born again by the regenerating action of the Holy Spirit we cannot please God—all our righteousness is "filthy rags" before him (Isaiah 64:6 KJV). First we are made new, then we live new lives by the empowering of the indwelling Holy Spirit. Only then can we have any realistic hope of living the holy life God calls his people to live.

QUESTION 46: What does it mean to "have no other gods before me"?

It means that we must acknowledge that there is one and only one true God, the LORD God of Israel, and not to let anything else whatsoever be more important to us.

The first commandment must be of special importance or it would surely not be first. We are told to have no other gods before the one, true, living God. This is a prohibition of idolatry, and we are told by Paul in Romans 1:21 that the failure to honour God as God and give thanks to him, is the root of all forms of idolatry. Idolatry is the root sin that leads to all other sin, according to Paul's analysis.

QUESTION 47: What does it mean to make "a carved image"?

It means to make an image of either the true God or a false god out of something physical and then to bow down to such images. We are to worship the LORD God alone.

In the second commandment we have a sort of "part two" of the prohibition of idolatry. The making of idols is rampant all over the world, and has been since earliest human history. The prohibition of bowing down to carved images is clearly understandable, but note that the prohibition extends even to the making of such images. As the people of God, we are to be entirely separate from the culture of idolatry that pervades the Gentile world. Millions of people have tried to excuse their idolatry by telling themselves that they really are worshipping God behind or through the idol itself. To forestall this excuse, God commands us not even to make an idol in the first place.

Note the vehemence with which God gives this commandment. He calls himself a *jealous* God who punishes idolatry severely. This punishment extends even to the children of the idolaters. Here we see the tragedy of idolatry: by engaging in idolatry you are even bringing God's wrath on your own children. We see this today when we watch, for example, a man place his career ahead of the best interests of his wife and children. The career becomes all-consuming, the marriage breaks up, the children suffer. Why? It is because of the immoral choice to commit idolatry in a peculiarly modern form.

When God punishes us, the reality is that because of the interconnectedness of the human family, there can be negative implications for those who depend on us to live godly lives. It can bring a string of heartbreaking consequences that result in sorrow, sadness, pain and dysfunction in the lives of those who depend on us. This is one reason why adultery is such a horrible, evil, destructive act.

QUESTION 48: What does it mean to "take the name of the LORD your God in vain"?

It means to use the name of God as a swear word or to invoke it carelessly.

J.I. Packer suggests that there are three ways to break this commandment: (1) irreverence; (2) bad language; and (3) promise-breaking. Words matter. They can damn us, and they can save us. Our society takes words lightly, but God takes them very seriously.

QUESTION 49: What does it mean to "remember the Sabbath day, to keep it holy"?

It means to use it for worship, rest and spiritual activities that draw us closer to God.

In the fourth commandment we are told to keep the Sabbath holy. The Ten Commandments are not the specific legislation God gave to Israel as the condition of being blessed in the Promised Land. It is not the civil law of Israel, which no longer applies to the church. It is also not the ceremonial law of the sacrificial system that was centred on the tabernacle/temple. That also is fulfilled in Jesus Christ's sacrificial death on the cross and no longer applicable to us today. The Ten Commandments are the republication of the eternal law of God. The Sabbath is rooted in creation, and the purpose of this command is to recognize the creation of the world by God and our consequent obligation to obey the moral law of God as seen in nature and human nature. Therefore, this is not a law specific to Christians or Jews; it is binding on everyone.

QUESTION 50: What does it mean to "honor your father and your mother"?

It means that we must obey all authorities placed over us by God with respect and humility, beginning with our parents and including teachers, employers and human governments. We are not, however, to obey any human authority that orders us to break one of God's commandments (Acts 4:19–20). We also honour parents by caring for them when they become old or sick.

The second tablet of the law (commandments 5 to 10) begins with the fifth commandment, that requires us to honour our father and mother. It is connected to Israel's endurance in the land, not because it is part of what I referred to as the civil law of Israel, but because this is true of any nation, in any land, in any century. The family is the basis of all human society and a society that fails to honour parents is a society that is in the process of declining and falling. This is true in the most literal sense imaginable; a society in which the family is destroyed cannot last.

The church has bought into a false teaching rampant in contemporary Western society: the exaltation of youth as the highest form of human life. The cult of youth has contributed to what Thomas E. Bergler has termed "the juvenilization" of Christianity.[2] This includes a tendency to despise and ignore the elderly. In all civilized cultures throughout history, elders have been accorded great respect, but this characteristic is missing from contemporary Western culture. The veneration of and respect for elders is part of a more general respect for all those in positions of authority—kings, government officials, employers, teachers and pastors. We cannot sustain a healthy society if we allow respect for authority to erode and decline.

QUESTION 51: What does it mean to commit murder?

Murder is taking human life intentionally and unlawfully. This does not include capital punishment or killing in a just war, which are not unlawful. It does include abortion, infanticide, euthanasia, suicide and all forms of private killing for evil motives such as convenience, revenge, robbery or hatred.

---

[2] Thomas E. Bergler, *The Juvenilization of American Christianity* (Grand Rapids: Eerdmans, 2012).

The sixth commandment is rightly translated *murder* not *kill*. The Bible would be contradicting itself if it said: "You shall not kill." The Bible clearly says in Ecclesiastes 3:3, there is "a time to kill, and a time to heal." God himself takes human life in judgement. When the state employs capital punishment and kills a murderer, it is not murder, and when a soldier kills another soldier in war, it is not murder. Killing an intruder in your home in self-defense is not murder. Murder is *unlawful* killing. It is killing for private reasons like revenge, robbery or intimidation. Murder is the deliberate, intentional killing of another human being by a private citizen in a way that is not sanctioned by divine law.

Note that even if the law of a given country legalizes killing, if that killing goes against natural law and the moral law of God, it is still murder. The laws of a human government cannot trump the law of God. The most obvious examples are abortion and euthanasia in Canada today. Another example from recent history is the laws passed in Germany that permitted the murder of Jewish people during the 1930s and 1940s simply for being Jewish. After World War 2, Nazi war criminals were hanged at Nuremberg for committing acts of murder that were technically legal in Germany when they happened. This punishment of so-called "legalized murder" was justice in accordance with the Ten Commandments. Legalized murder is still murder in God's eyes.

In society today, there has been a relaxation of the law against self-murder or suicide. Suicide is no longer illegal, and many people have come to believe that one has some sort of "right" to take one's own life. But if life is a gift from God, it is not ours to dispose of as we wish. The rise of euthanasia is a key sign of the culture of death, and it reflects a society that has lost its fear of God and its respect for human life made in the image of God.

QUESTION 52: What does it mean to commit adultery?

It means to break the marriage covenant and thereby to destroy the family. This commandment prohibits all forms of sexual activity outside of heterosexual, permanent, procreative marriage, including fornication, homosexuality, incest, bestiality, pornography and all other forms of sexual immorality.

The seventh commandment forbids sexual activity outside of marriage and is the foundation of a stable family structure. Adultery here means basically any sexual activity that goes against the will of God by violating the marriage covenant. The purpose of human sexuality is made clear in nature itself, and the will of God is clearly revealed in Genesis 1–2 and emphasized by Jesus himself in Matthew 19:3–9. Of all the human bodily systems, only the reproductive system does not function as a complete unit for each individual human being. Our nervous system, digestive system, circulatory system and so on all function as a complete unit and do the job they were designed to do in a single individual person. But the reproductive system is incomplete and incapable of achieving its purpose in a single person. Only when there is a joining together of two people in the act of marriage can the reproductive system be completed and accomplish its purpose. Only within committed marriage can the fruit of the sexual act—children—be raised in an optimal environment designed to allow them to flourish. This is why sex is obviously designed for marriage; any rational creature not blinded by stubborn willfulness or led astray by out-of-control passions, can see that reality.

Our contemporary world is completely confused about the purpose of pleasure in human sexuality. The purpose is clearly to drive people toward marriage and sexual union. Only a few acts of marriage actually result in conception. The woman is not capable of conceiving a child two thirds of the time, yet sexual desire is constant. The natural sex drive draws the couple together in love and mutuality for a lifetime. The unitive purpose of sex naturally complements the procreative purpose so that marriage is enhanced by sexual desire as long as the desire is guided by the rational mind and is not allowed to spiral out of control. This permanent, monogamous union provides the ideal environment for the conception, birth, nurturing and raising of new human beings.

Since the sexual revolution of the 1960s, our society has attempted to separate sex from procreation and family by making selfish, individual, pleasurable sensations the main purpose of sex, rather than procreation and child raising. Adultery is a crime against children, the spouse and society as a whole. It is a great wickedness, and God hates it and is determined to punish it severely. Those who commit this sin will feel its effects for generations to come, even if the individual does repent and find forgiveness. Its effects cannot easily be undone even when a person desperately wants to do so.

QUESTION 53: What does it mean to steal?

It means to take anything that does not belong to us. We may steal in many ways, including outright robbery or theft, but also by failing to fulfil contracts and other obligations.

The eighth commandment is one that makes life in society possible and one that is indispensable for any civilization. The principle is simple and clear: do not take what belongs to someone else. The problem is that because of sin, human ingenuity is often focused on finding creative ways to steal. People, for some strange reason, would rather work at finding ways to steal from others than working at earning wealth. This reflects our depravity and makes little sense. This is another example of how sin makes people stupid.

The implicit premise contained in this commandment is the existence and validity of private property. If there were no private property there could not be theft. But private property is a fundamental assumption of civilization, and it is closely correlated to freedom. All totalitarian governments launch an all-out assault on private property. Excessive levels of laws and regulations can do the same thing as outright nationalization of property. The less government owns outright and/or controls, the freer the citizens of that country are.

> **QUESTION 54:** What does it mean to "bear false witness against your neighbor"?
>
> It means to tell an untruth intended to harm another person. Our word should be our bond, and we must be honest in our words and dealings.

The ninth commandment forbids theft by lying. We owe each other the truth. This commandment is most often broken when we covet and wish to steal that which belongs to our neighbour. We can steal goods or money, or we can steal reputation, by slander or defamation. We can do this from malice or greed or simply from a desire to make ourselves look good. We owe others the truth, and there are very few circumstances when it is right to withhold the truth. Much of the time we find it easier not to tell the truth, especially when we believe the truth will not be well-received by the person involved.

> **QUESTION 55:** What does it mean to covet?
>
> It means to lust after things that belong to our neighbour. We are to be content with what God has given us.

The tenth commandment says we should not covet what belongs to our neighbour. It is interesting that this commandment, which refers to an internal condition of our heart and mind, rather than to an outward action like stealing or murder or even Sabbath-keeping, is in this list. Sometimes it is said that the Old Testament law was only a matter of external actions, whereas the New Testament deals with heart attitudes as well. However, this is only a generalization and not entirely accurate. Here, just as in the first commandment, we are dealing with heart attitudes.

Merely to want to have what is not ours is wrong. Why? There are at least two reasons. First, it shows our sinful nature in not being content. The opposite of covetousness is contentedness. Second, it is a way of nursing the intent to sin, and often leads to the breaking of other commandments.

CONCLUSION

When we observe the structure of the Ten Commandments, we note that the first and tenth ones deal with heart attitudes, while the second and eighth commandments deal with outward actions of making idols and stealing. The first and tenth ones forbid idolatry in the heart and coveting that which belongs to someone else. It is simply not true that the Old Testament law only deals with outward, external actions, while the New Testament deals with internal heart attitudes. To keep God's law as God intends is to be committed to God's will in both our thoughts and our actions. The Ten Commandments reveal the eternal, moral law of God to poor, miserable sinners so there can be no doubt about the standard of God for judgement. We have a summary of laws to hold civil society, together and we can measure our progress in holiness as Christians. Like the psalmist, we should love the law of God and treasure it in our hearts.

Questions for reflection

1. What are some good ways to keep the Sabbath day?

2. On what theological basis is suicide prohibited?

3. In what sense can fornication (sexual relations between unmarried persons) be said to be breaking the marriage covenant?

11

Why do we celebrate the Lord's Supper?

PART V
The Lord's Supper—Christian Worship
QUESTIONS 56–63

"The Lord's Supper is the gospel enacted in signs."

INTRODUCTION

We now come to the fifth section of the catechism, which deals with the central act of Christian worship, namely, the Lord's Supper. At the time of the Reformation in the sixteenth century, the main points of doctrine in dispute were not the doctrines of the Trinity or the two natures of Christ, but rather doctrines relating to how we are saved (justification by faith alone by grace alone) and the nature of the church (the relationship of the hierarchy, the priesthood and the sacraments). The root issues had to do with the legalism that had crept into late medieval theology and the exaggerated emphasis on the power of the pope and bishops to control the dispensing of grace to ordinary people through the sacrifice of the mass, which could only be offered by the priest under the authority of the bishop. Making things worse was the tendency of the Renaissance popes to meddle far too much in politics and war, and the lack of truly holy men in key offices, including the papacy itself. The overall appearance of the church at the end of the Middle Ages was a human institution seeking to control the dispensing of grace for secular, political ends by means of legalism and power politics. All this was very far from the spiritual mission of the church to preach the gospel and bring sinners into a saving relationship with God. There was a widespread sense in European Christendom that something was desperately wrong and reform was needed.

But reform alone was not all that was needed. Spiritual renewal was necessary as well, if the health of the church was to be restored and the central mission of the church to be accomplished. Let us define these two words: reform and renewal. *Reform* refers to going back to Scripture and tradition in order to get rid of the distortions introduced over time by heretics. Reform means altering church structures in accordance with sound doctrine and reconsidering the relationship of the church to the secular society around it. We could think of reform as mainly a matter of the *head*. *Renewal*, on the other hand, is mainly a matter of the *heart*. It involves lethargic saints being stirred up with holy zeal for the things of God. It involves people being converted for the first time to a personal, living faith in Christ or backslidden Christians being revived by a fresh moving of the Spirit. In church renewal there is a return to the basics of prayer, confession of sin, brokenness before God and surrender to God's will. What we call the Reformation in the sixteenth century actually was both a movement of renewal and one of reform.

Evangelicalism emerged through the eighteenth-century revivals led by John Wesley and George Whitefield, but it had roots in the Puritan and Pietist movements of the seventeenth century. These movements originated in Protestant churches where there was too much dead orthodoxy and too little spiritual vitality. Evangelicalism is primarily a movement of renewal in the Western church that seeks to complete the work of the Reformation by standing on sound, Reformed doctrine and preaching personal conversion and discipleship on the basis of Protestant doctrine.

As we come to the Lord's Supper and consider its role in the worship of the church, we need to examine the meaning of the Lord's Supper and the benefits we derive from it. We also need to examine how to approach it correctly so as not to bring judgement on ourselves. In the Lord's Supper, we receive the strength we need for the journey of the Christian life through meditating on Jesus Christ, who gave his body for us on the cross. As we do so, we become increasingly united to him by faith, and he increasingly lives in and through us by the power of the Holy Spirit.

I. THE LORD'S SUPPER AS THE HEART
OF CHRISTIAN WORSHIP

QUESTION 56: What is the heart of Christian worship?

Worship includes many elements, including praise, confession and prayer. But the heart of Christian worship is the proclamation of the gospel by two means: the preaching of the Word and the celebration of the two ordinances or sacraments given by our Lord as visible signs of the gospel, namely, baptism and the Lord's Supper.

The sacraments visibly enact the gospel, and preaching explains the meaning of the sacraments in words. Together, the preached Word and enacted sacraments declare the gospel by the power of the Holy Spirit.

Every worship service ought to be carefully planned to focus on the gospel. The gospel is what makes the church the church. The Reformers taught that the church exists wherever the gospel is rightly preached and the sacraments rightly administered. This was Martin Luther's definition of the church. Calvin and the Reformed tradition added a third essential mark: church discipline. The church, then, is the gathered community of disciples who have personally confessed Christ in baptism, feed regularly at the Lord's Table and are faithful in weekly worship.

The reason the Reformers mentioned both the preaching of the gospel and the proper administration of the sacraments is that baptism and the Lord's Supper picture the gospel in a graphic and profound manner. Both preaching and the sacraments are ways of declaring the gospel—the sacraments visually portray the gospel, and preaching explains and expounds the gospel. We have already seen that baptism is the means by which Christians confess their personal faith in Jesus Christ and demonstrate that they have been converted by repentance and faith. Baptism is, therefore, the sacrament of *conversion,* and the Lord's Supper is the sacrament of *discipleship*.

In the Great Commission, Jesus told his disciples to make disciples, baptize and teach (Matthew 28:19–20). The teaching part refers to discipleship. The process of making disciples begins with conversion and is symbolized by the *one-time* sacrament of baptism. This process continues throughout a believer's life through teaching and growth in grace and is symbolized by the *oft-repeated* sacrament of the Lord's Supper.

The Lord's Supper is a picture of continual dying to self and union with Christ that is characteristic of the true Christian life. For this reason, it is the centre of the worship of the church. We worship God by enacting, declaring and confessing the gospel week by week throughout our lives. In so doing we fulfil the Great Commission of our Lord and are gradually transformed into the image of Christ.

The Christian life is more than "head knowledge" of certain biblical facts—it is a new life in which we die progressively to our old nature and live in an ever-intensifying way in Christ. Worship is meant to draw us more and more into union with Christ so that we can increasingly mortify (or kill) the flesh while drawing our life increasingly from the Spirit of Christ who indwells us.

Worship is where we focus on God and his grace, but we need to understand that doing so is transformative. The real reason many people do not wish to worship God is that they do not want to die to their fleshly lusts and be changed into the image of Christ, who is totally submissive to the Father. They simply don't wish to be totally submissive to the Father. They want to submit to their own fleshly desires and enjoy "the pleasures of sin for a season," as the King James Version so graphically states it (Hebrews 11:25). The Lord's Supper brings us into the closest communion with Christ that is possible on this earth. Jesus Christ is personally present in every communion service ready to meet you, change you, kill your sinful, fleshly nature and make you alive by the power of his resurrection. Do you fear to meet him?

II. THE MEANING OF THE LORD'S SUPPER

Questions 57–63 explain the nature and the meaning of the Lord's Supper. We will discuss the contents of these questions under three main headings: What is going on in communion? In what sense is Christ present in the Supper? How should we prepare for the Supper?

1. What is going on in communion?

QUESTION 57: What is the Lord's Supper?

The Lord's Supper (also known as Communion or the Eucharist) is one of the two ordinances or sacraments of the church, which we perform in obedience to the command of our Lord Jesus Christ. In the Lord's Supper we eat the bread and drink of the cup as a celebration of thanksgiving for Christ's death, an experience of our union with him and as a proclamation of his death until he comes again.

Here we see that there are two alternate names given for the Lord's Supper: Communion and Eucharist. These two names describe two of the most important things that happen in the Lord's Supper.

Communion is a term often used to describe the Lord's Supper in the New Testament. It is a word that expresses the kind of fellowship the church has with Christ. It is the same word as the one from which we get the word *community*. Unfortunately, community is a desperately over-worked word today, and its common meaning has been drastically watered down. Every imaginable group of people with even one thing in common is referred to as a community today. But when we speak of communion or community in the New Testament sense, we are speaking of a miraculous creation of God. The church is not merely a human community brought into being by human will. Rather, it is a divine miracle brought into being by the miraculous grace of God as displayed in the power that raised Jesus from the dead. Communion in this New Testament sense is an ontological reality, not merely a projection of the human mind. It is an existing reality independent of our thoughts or will. Communion really exists as a spiritual reality, capable of influencing the material world. The communion of the saints is made possible by our union with Christ. The church is the body of Christ, and each member is one with him and with each other.

Eucharist comes from the Greek verb used in the New Testament meaning "to give thanks." A eucharist is a ceremony centred on thanksgiving. In Romans, Paul identifies the root of pagan idolatry and sin as the refusal to give thanks: "For although they knew God, they did not honor him as God or give thanks to him, but they became futile in their thinking, and their foolish hearts were darkened" (Romans 1:21). The precise opposite of pagan idolatry is the Christian eucharist. When the church gathers weekly to worship God, at the centre of its worship is *thanksgiving* to God—and nowhere does this thanksgiving become more obvious than in the Lord's Supper. The root of the worship of the true God is thankfulness, which is the opposite of the root of idolatry, which is ingratitude toward the Creator.

The next three questions describe the institution of the Lord's Supper in the New Testament.

QUESTION 58: When was the first Lord's Supper?

It took place on the night before Jesus was crucified, when Jesus commanded his disciples, "Do this in remembrance of me" (Luke 22:14–23; Matthew 26:26–29).

> **QUESTION 59:** What is the significance of the bread?
>
> Jesus took bread and broke it and said: "This is my body, which is given for you" (Luke 22:19).

Christ offered his body as a sacrifice on the cross for us—on our behalf—in order to reconcile us to God.

> **QUESTION 60:** What is the significance of the cup?
>
> Jesus took the cup after supper saying: "Drink of it, all of you, for this is my blood of the covenant, which is poured out for many for the forgiveness of sins" (Matthew 26:27–28).

Note the key words "blood of the covenant." Jesus's blood, symbolizing his death on the cross, is the basis of the New Covenant.

Now we consider the meaning of these sacred words and actions of our Lord Jesus Christ. What is going on in the Lord's Supper, or Communion or the Eucharist? We might think of it as having three dimensions that we can see by looking in three directions.

a. The look back: the Lord's Supper as remembrance

The Lord's Supper is first of all an act of remembrance of the past. In the Passover meal, the children of Israel were commanded to remember the great act of divine deliverance from Egypt. Just so, the Christian community is commanded to remember the great act of deliverance accomplished by Jesus in fulfilment of the Old Testament prophecies. The cross and resurrection of Christ is the reality of which the Exodus was a type. Jesus is our Passover Lamb: as John the Baptist said: "Behold, the Lamb of God, who takes away the sin of the world!" (John 1:29).

But the meaning of the word *remembrance* here is not merely to recall to our minds something that is past and therefore not currently real. The meaning is stronger than that. When we remember Jesus Christ in the Lord's Supper, the Holy Spirit makes the effects of that past event real here and now in us. The act of human remembering is merely the reception of the real act of God in the here and now. It is primarily God's act, not merely a human act. Jesus is alive and real today, right here. He is not dead, and he is not merely past. He is alive and able to change you and me. In the

Lord's Supper the power of his resurrection becomes real to us and we receive grace and power to grow and change into the image of Jesus Christ.

b. The look around: the Lord's Supper as thanksgiving and communion

Second, in the Lord's Supper we take a look around as we consider what it means to be part of Christ's body, the church. The communion we experience in the Lord's Supper has a double reference. We are in communion with Christ, and we are in communion with the other members of his body: "we who are many are one body, for we all partake of the one bread" (1 Corinthians 10:17). We have sweet communion with one another because of our communion with Christ. Insofar are we are part of his body, we are members one of another. Further, this realization that we are in communion with Christ and his church should prompt us to be thankful for all that Christ has done for us and in us and to us: "when he had given thanks…" (Mark 14:23). We give thanks for salvation from sin, for peace with God and for the comfort of the Holy Spirit.

The most basic level of our salvation is our union with Christ. We are made one with him by call, regeneration, conversion, adoption and justification. Our union with Christ is the reason why sanctification happens. To be united with Christ is to have the Spirit of Christ living in us and thus to be "in Christ." To be in Christ is to live with a heart of gratitude.

c. The look forward: the Lord's Supper as anticipation of the second coming

Third, in the Lord's Supper we look forward in anticipation of the Second Coming of our Lord and Saviour Jesus Christ: "I tell you I will not drink again of this fruit of the vine until that day when I drink it new with you in my Father's kingdom" (Matthew 26:29). Jesus wanted to reassure his disciples at the last supper that his impending death on the cross was not going to be the end of his ministry. He wanted to give them hope at that darkest hour of their lives. As we gather around the table of the Lord we proclaim hope to one another as we look forward to the return of the Lord.

2. In what sense is Christ present in the Supper?

Questions 61–63 inform us about how Christ is active in the Supper.

QUESTION 61: Is it just a memorial of a past event?

No, it is that and more. It is a remembrance of the death of Christ and the great love of God who sent his Son to die for us while we were still his enemies (Romans 5:8). However, since Christ is alive we can also expect him to meet us in the Supper and impart grace to us so that we can be strengthened for the Christian life.

QUESTION 62: What can we expect the risen Lord Jesus Christ to do when he meets us in the Lord's Supper through his Holy Spirit?

We can expect him to sanctify us by uniting us to him ever more closely. Specifically, we can expect three things: first, comfort in our afflictions, second, conviction of how we need to grow in grace, and third, strength to live the Christian life.

If we have been saved by faith, we are united to Christ, but we can grow in our consciousness of that union. We can also expect to receive the nourishment we need to live the Christian life through his comfort, conviction and strength.

QUESTION 63: How does the Lord's Supper differ from baptism?

Baptism is the sacrament of the beginning of the Christian life, and we undergo it only once, whereas the Lord's Supper is the sacrament of the continuation of the Christian life, and we partake of it frequently for our spiritual benefit. Baptism is a picture of our regeneration by the Holy Spirit and justification by faith alone, whereas the Lord's Supper is a picture of our on-going sanctification and hope of resurrection.

Baptism is a picture of the beginning of the Christian life, which starts when we are born again and regenerated by the Holy Spirit. It is appropriate that baptism is something we experience passively (we are baptized) because we do not save ourselves but are saved by the grace of God. The Lord's Supper is a picture of the continuation of the Christian life, and we must take the bread and the cup (we extend the empty hand of faith) in order to grow in sanctifying grace.

As we have seen already, the biblical teaching is that Jesus Christ is alive and active in the world today by his Holy Spirit. He is not dead or inactive, but living and powerful and at work in his church. It is important to understand that we are not talking merely about him being alive in our memories—it is a stronger sense than that. In a materialistic culture like ours, to say that Jesus is alive in a spiritual sense sounds like he is not really real. But in the biblical worldview, reality has two parts: the spiritual and the material, and they are not disconnected. Jesus' spiritual presence is a *real* presence.

In the biblical worldview, there is a spiritual realm of angels, heaven and the risen Christ, but this is not simply spiritual. Jesus' resurrected *body* is in heaven, and angels have often appeared in our material world in *physical* form. It is probably better to think of the spiritual realm as a perfected version of our material realm, where the solidity and reality of our world is preserved, while some of the limitations of our world are transcended. One day, our physical world will be unified with heaven and transformed and perfected as a result (Revelation 21–22).

With that as background, we must acknowledge that Christians have debated the exact manner of Christ's presence in the Supper for centuries. From the New Testament to the late Middle Ages, the church was agreed that Christ's presence in the Supper was in some sense real. This period also witnessed the emergence of a sacramental priesthood controlling the sacraments. In this situation, some theologians claimed to be able to explain the mode of Christ's presence by means of the doctrine of *transubstantiation*. In this theory, the bread and the wine were transformed into the *actual* body and blood of Christ at the moment of priestly consecration. Outwardly (in their "accidents") they appeared to be ordinary bread and wine, but in their essence they were now actually the very body and blood of Christ. Transubstantiation is one way of thinking of Christ as really present in his Supper, but it is not the only way.

The Reformers associated this medieval theory of Christ's presence with the sacramental priesthood and the control of God's grace by a human institution and thus rejected it. But they were unable to agree among themselves as to the nature of Christ's presence in the Supper. Luther developed a theory quite similar to the Roman Catholic view, while Zwingli went to the opposite extreme and practically rejected the real presence of Christ in the Supper altogether. He claimed that the Supper is just a memorial meal—Christ is only present insofar as we remember him. If the Roman Catholics and Luther tend to make Christ too material, Zwingli and the Anabaptists tend to make him too unreal. Calvin was in the middle on this issue, affirming a real, spiritual presence as the church had done for the first thousand years of its existence.

The main problem with the Reformed view (Calvin's view) is that today the word "spiritual" has the unfortunate connotation of "unreal" or "merely in the mind." He meant much more than that. In order to understand the meaning of Christ's real, spiritual presence in the Supper, we need to think of it as having real effects in our material world. Christ can actually change your life: he can convict you of sin, give you victory over temptation, provide guidance for your life, strengthen you for spiritual warfare, create contentment in you and give your life purpose and meaning. Christ is really present in the Supper, and he wants to change your life.

3. How should we prepare for the Supper?

Paul writes in 1 Corinthians 11:27: "Whoever, therefore, eats the bread or drinks the cup of the Lord in an unworthy manner will be guilty concerning the body and blood of the Lord." Here, Paul urges us to examine ourselves prior to Communion to ensure that all sin has been confessed and cleansed so that we are ready to participate worthily.

Do not be confused by what is meant here by *worthily*. We participate worthily when we are *repentant*, not when we are *sinless*. Nobody is worthy in the sense of being totally without sin. Every person who comes to the table of the Lord is a sinner, and some have sinned very recently. If only people who had not sinned recently came, there might be very few taking communion. The important thing is that no one comes to the table with unconfessed sin. To do that is to despise the body and blood of Christ. It is to make light of our salvation and to mock the holy sacrifice of our Lord on our behalf.

Nineteenth-century Baptists in Nova Scotia and New Brunswick had a covenant renewal service on the Saturday night prior to the Sunday when Communion was scheduled. These Baptist churches had a church covenant, and they took that covenant seriously. The service provided time for prayer, meditation and self-examination based on the covenant obligations the members had freely adopted by virtue of joining the church. It was an opportunity to get right with God and, sometimes, an opportunity to get right with each other before Communion. This is the kind of seriousness that Paul is speaking of in 1 Corinthians 11.

CONCLUSION

The Lord's Supper is the heart of Christian worship because it brings us face to face with the risen, living Lord Jesus Christ, who is the focus of all worship. It is the ongoing sacrament of discipleship that keeps us focused on the broken body and shed blood of Christ, which is the basis of our salvation and our only hope of escaping judgement. As we partake of the Lord's Supper, we feed on him and receive grace and strength to live the Christian life. As we approach the Lord's Table, we expect to meet none other than the Lord himself—alive and in person. It is not just a ritual when we approach it in living faith—it is an encounter with the risen Lord, and it brings us into ever-closer and ever-increasing union with him, whom to know rightly is life eternal.

Questions for reflection

1. Why did the church need reform in the sixteenth century? What was the unique, historical mission of Evangelicalism as a movement? Is that mission still needed today?

2. According to Calvin, what are the three marks of the true church? How do you recognize a true church?

3. What are the two aspects of communion that we experience in the Lord's Supper?

4. In what sense is Christ present in the Lord's Supper? What two extremes are avoided in the Reformed doctrine of the real spiritual presence?

5. How should we prepare for Communion?

12

How should Christians pray?

PART VI
The Lord's Prayer—Christian Spirituality
QUESTIONS 64–77

"The Lord's Prayer shows us what true prayer is."

INTRODUCTION

We now come to the sixth part of the catechism: the Lord's Prayer. We will briefly consider the purpose, structure and content of the Lord's Prayer. This prayer is densely packed with spiritual truth and rewards careful study, memorization, meditation and frequent use in both private and public worship. The teaching contained in this prayer is the key to Christian spirituality. If we let this prayer sink into our consciousness and shape the way we think, it will shape our worldview in such a way that we will begin to think like Christ and relate to our heavenly Father in the way that Jesus did while on earth. We will develop a God-centred view of the world.

I. THE PURPOSE OF THE PRAYER

First, we look at Questions 64–66 of the catechism, where we learn what the Lord's Prayer is and how we are to make use of it.

> **QUESTION 64:** What is the Lord's Prayer?
>
> ___
>
> It is the prayer our Lord Jesus taught his disciples to say (Matthew 6:9–13).

Jesus taught this prayer to his disciples in response to their request that he teach them to pray. Do you wish to learn from Jesus himself how to pray? Then it makes sense to pay special attention to this prayer. This is why we memorize the Lord's Prayer—we want it to be in our minds at all times so that it comes to shape our thinking about prayer and shape the actual prayers we pray.

> **QUESTION 65:** Are we to say it too?
>
> ___
>
> Yes, we should commit it to memory and let it form the structure of prayers in both worship services and our private prayers. Saying it aloud in worship services reminds us of the proper content and structure of prayer. Reciting it can also give us comfort when we do not know how to pray in our own words due to discouragement, sickness or distress.

> **QUESTION 66:** What does this prayer say?
>
> ___
>
> "Our Father in heaven, hallowed be your name. Your kingdom come, your will be done, on earth as it is in heaven. Give us this day our daily bread, and forgive us our debts, as we also have forgiven our debtors. And lead us not into temptation, but deliver us from evil. For yours is the kingdom and the power and the glory, forever. Amen" (Matthew 6:9–13 alt).

Jesus explicitly told his disciples that they should pray in this way: "Pray then like this" (v.9). The natural question that arises is: What does it mean to "pray like this"? Does it mean repeating the exact words? Does it mean making the themes of this prayer central in our praying? Does it mean structuring our prayers according to this basic pattern? The answer is: All of the above. Repeating these exact words will burn the pattern and themes into our memory. These patterns then become the form our own prayers take and eventually become second nature to us. We should take care in our public prayers to structure them according to the pattern of the Lord's Prayer because in public prayers we are providing, whether we realize it or not, examples for people to follow in their private prayers.

II. THE STRUCTURE OF THE PRAYER

QUESTION 67: How is this prayer structured?

It is divided into two parts with three petitions focused on the person of God, followed by three petitions focused on our bodily and spiritual needs.

The prayer has a very definite structure as we can see from the chart on the following page. There is one overwhelming feature of this structure that makes this prayer distinctively Christian and totally different from most other prayer in the world. It is God-focused.

QUESTION 68: What is the significance of this structure for our prayer life?

If we want to experience blessing, we ought first to focus our attention on God and his faithfulness before we bring our needs before him. This practice increases our faith in him.

The basic structure of the prayer shows that God has priority and is central. Prayer begins with God. If we want to experience blessing, we ought first to focus our attention on God and his faithfulness before we bring our needs before him. This practice increases our faith in him.

The God-centredness of prayer is what makes prayer distinctively Christian. Christian prayer is theocentric, not human-centred. Human needs have a place in Christian prayer, just not the central place.

A practical benefit of theocentric prayer is that it just happens to be the

ANALYSIS OF THE LORD'S PRAYER

The Lord's Prayer trains us to focus on God before turning to our own requests, needs and concerns.

Intro	Our Father in heaven,	Focus on the One to whom we pray
First half	**3 petitions**	**FOCUS ON GOD**
1st petition	Hallowed be your name.	Recognition of God's holiness
2nd petition	Your kingdom come,	Longing for God's kingdom
3rd petition	Your will be done, on earth as it is in heaven.	Submission to God's will
Second half	**3 petitions**	**FOCUS ON US**
4th petition	Give us this day our daily bread,	Our physical needs
5th petition	And forgive us our debts, as we also have forgiven our debtors.	Our need for forgiveness
6th petition	And lead us not into temptation, but deliver us from evil.	Our need for protection

case that the more we focus on God the more our faith increases. Conversely, the more we focus on ourselves the more our faith evaporates. We must have faith if we wish to have our prayers answered, and Jesus teaches us here exactly how to go about increasing our faith. It is paradoxical that the more God-centred we are, the more our human needs will be met. This suggests that the universe has a built-in order and structure, and theocentric prayer that results in human beings being blessed is good because it fits with the basic order and structure of reality.

The idea that there might be more than mere chance in the structure of the Lord's Prayer is reinforced by the fact that there is a direct parallel between the structure of the prayer and the Ten Commandments. Both are divided into two parts with the first part focused on God and the second part focused on humanity. Both make a place for love of neighbour and our own personal needs, but both put the glory, honour and sovereignty of God in first place. Both are theocentric.

III. THE CONTENT OF THE PRAYER

QUESTION 69: Why does it begin with "Our Father in heaven"?

We begin by addressing God as "Our Father" because Jesus Christ is God's Son, and we have been adopted as sons of God by virtue of being in Christ. Therefore, God is our Father, and we can come to him as his beloved children with all our cares and burdens.

We are obeying our Lord Jesus's instructions by addressing God as "Our Father." Jesus is God's Son and, insofar as we are *in him* by virtue of being saved, we are also sons and daughters of God along with him. Adoption entitles us to come directly into God's presence and makes it reasonable to look to him to meet all our needs as a father cares for his children.

The prayer begins with a focus on God. Note also that the first two phrases do not constitute a petition. We begin not with our needs but by shifting our attention from our needs to God, from earth to heaven, from us to our Father. This is the key to all true prayer—it must begin with a focus on God.

We are taught by Jesus to use this personal designation for God: Father. In no other religion in the world are people taught to address God in this way. We approach Jesus as the children of our heavenly Father. Why? We have been united to Christ through baptism, and so we are one with him, and he is the eternal Son of the Father. We share in the Son's sonship as the adopted sons and daughters of God. He is Son by nature, but we are sons and daughters by adoption. Nevertheless, when it comes to communication with God we are commanded by our Lord to address him as our heavenly Father.

QUESTION 70: What does "hallowed be your name" mean?

It expresses our desire that God's name be lifted high and glorified. God's name stands for his person and character.

True prayer begins by reminding ourselves of who God is. Because of who God is we can trust him to meet our needs and do what is best for us. We do not have to worry that he lacks the *power* to accomplish his will, and we do not have to worry that he is not totally and unalterably *good*. We can put our trust in God in a way that we cannot put it in anyone or anything else.

The focus on God continues with the first three petitions. In this first petition, we begin by turning our focus toward God, but not to just any god. Specifically, we focus on God our loving, heavenly Father who will not disappoint us. But even then, we are taught to restrain ourselves and not blurt out our petitions immediately. When human children approach their earthly father, they often babble on immediately and without hesitation about whatever it is they want. But we are to be well-mannered and polite children who have learned self-control in the presence of our heavenly Father. Instead of rushing into a litany of our needs and desires, Jesus teaches us to pray that God's name be hallowed. Before we are allowed to mention our needs, we are first taught to focus on God's name, God's kingdom and God's will.

We are told here to pray that God's name be hallowed. In the world today, God's name is used more often than not as a swear word—carelessly, irreverently and thoughtlessly. The third commandment says: "You shall not take the name of the Lord your God in vain" (Exodus 20:7). This commandment is broken continuously every day, yet we are told to pray for God's name to be hallowed.

One day this prayer will be answered and God's name will be hallowed everywhere on earth. In the meantime, the church lifts up God's holy name in prayer during worship. It would be wonderful if the name of God could be uttered reverently in prayer and worship more times than it is desecrated on a daily basis in our world. John Piper, in his book on missions, has wisely written, "Mission exists because worship doesn't."[1] We preach the gospel, make disciples and do evangelistic and missionary work because, ultimately, we desire that God's name be hallowed everywhere by everyone.

QUESTION 71: What does it mean to ask for God's kingdom to "come"?

It means that we are to look forward to the blessed appearing of our Lord and Saviour Jesus Christ, who will judge the world in righteousness and set up his glorious kingdom (Titus 2:13; Psalm 96).

One day the kingdom of God will come upon the earth—that will be a great and glorious day! But many Christians are confused about what the kingdom of God is. The kingdom is not something we bring about on earth by

---

[1] John Piper, *Let the Nations Be Glad! The Supremacy of God in Missions*, 2nd ed. (Grand Rapids: Baker Academic, 2003), 17.

our efforts or work. It is not a human political project. It is something that already exists in heaven, and it will come to earth only when Christ returns. Our job is to be witnesses to the coming kingdom, not to think that we can build it on earth by human efforts. This does not mean we should not try to help those who are poor, sick or elderly or work to save the unborn and handicapped. We should try to repeal unjust laws and improve society wherever possible. But we should have no illusions about turning a fallen world into the kingdom of God by means at our disposal here and now.

QUESTION 72: What does it mean for God's "will to be done, on earth as it is in heaven"?

It means that we long for justice and for the righting of all wrongs and for God to put the world right.

We should long for justice to be done and for all wrongs to be reversed—for good to be rewarded and for evil to be punished. This is the flip side of saying that men and women are not able to build the kingdom of God on earth. The good news is that *God* can and will do it—in his good time, at the right time, according to his plan.

Heaven can be defined as that place where God's will is done perfectly and God's presence is unmediated. We are to pray that God's perfect will will someday be done perfectly on earth as it is in heaven. One day that will be true—and on that day the kingdom of God will have come. This will only happen once Jesus returns. In this world there is no final justice—only partial, tentative justice. We should strive to see justice done, but we know that only the Second Coming of Christ and the reign of the Son of God upon the earth will bring perfect justice.

The next three petitions turn from a focus on God's name, God's will and God's kingdom to a focus on our needs.

QUESTION 73: What does it mean to ask God for our "daily bread"?

It means that we are to depend on and trust God for all our physical needs including food, shelter and clothing.

Here at last we come to the place where our desires and needs are designed to fit. Here we are taught to bring our requests before God in humility, with confidence that he knows our needs and will care for us as his beloved children. We are taught to pray for our daily bread even though we may have a very good idea where that bread is coming from because we picked up a loaf of bread at the grocery story yesterday. Why should we pray this way? Because we are to train ourselves to think of God as providing for us even when the way he does so is to give us the health and strength to work and earn a living. It is God who has given us a job, allowed us to keep that job and blessed us with a country in which food is readily available at a reasonable cost. All this is from him.

QUESTION 74: What does it mean to pray, "forgive us our debts, as we also have forgiven our debtors"?

It means that we ought to be ever-conscious of our sins and ready to confess them before our loving, heavenly Father so that we can be forgiven and so that all impediments to spiritual communion with him can be removed.

This petition reminds us that we ought to forgive others because of our relationship to our heavenly Father, who has forgiven us through Christ. The clear implication is that when we do not forgive others there is an obstacle to our communion with God. While the fourth petition concerns the needs of our bodies, this petition concerns the needs of our souls. Our greatest *bodily* need is food and drink, without which we cannot survive physically. Our greatest *spiritual* need is for forgiveness, without which we cannot survive eternally. All of us are sinners by nature and by choice and very few of us live in a constant state of surrender to the Holy Spirit. Christians are people who know they need God's forgiveness and who repent regularly and trust in divine mercy rather than in personal goodness.

QUESTION 75: What is a sure sign of this spiritual communion with the Father?

If we have truly experienced forgiveness of our sins by our heavenly Father, we will be able and willing to extend forgiveness to those who have wronged us.

When our heavenly Father forgives us, he makes it possible for us to forgive others. It is simply impossible for the one who has truly experienced God's forgiveness to fail to forgive those by whom they have been wronged. To experience God's forgiveness changes us in ways we cannot control (which is why some people are afraid of it), and we find ourselves doing things (like forgiving our enemies) that we never envisioned ourselves doing before we had this experience.

Can we be forgiven without forgiving? I would suggest that the natural man, apart from the empowerment of the Spirit of Christ, finds it impossible to forgive in certain situations. How can we forgive the injustices others do if we believe they are getting off scot-free? How can we let go of injustice if we do not believe in a final Day of Judgement when all evil will be punished and all good rewarded? How can we not claim justice for ourselves—which is what it means to refuse to forgive—when we think that justice will never be done? We could only do that by giving up on justice altogether. That would be to sink into despair and cease to be fully human.

It is only belief in the final, perfect, comprehensive justice of God that allows us to forgive without despair. And when we believe, by the grace of the Holy Spirit, in the future Day of Judgement, we finally realize that justice does not depend on us, but wholly on God. The man who is able to forgive his enemies is not weak, nor is he giving up on justice. No, on the contrary, the man who can forgive his enemies is strong in the Lord and can do so only because he believes in a justice that is higher, more certain and more perfect than human justice—including that which we might desire to mete out—could ever be. Therefore, to be able to forgive is a sign that we are saved and our worldview has been transformed by the experience of grace.

QUESTION 76: What does it mean to ask that we not be led "into temptation" but delivered "from evil"?

It means that we rely on God's protection as we journey through this dangerous world as pilgrims on our way to our heavenly home.

This world is not our home—we are pilgrims looking for a better country! We live in the middle of a spiritual war and it is only our spiritual lethargy that prevents us from being more sensitive to the attacks of Satan and the dangers around us. Everywhere we turn, we face the lies, temptations and deceptions of Satan. Only by prayer, watchfulness and dependence on the Spirit of God can we hope to be protected from the spiritual dangers surrounding us.

QUESTION 77: What does the conclusion of the prayer, "For yours is the kingdom and the power and the glory, forever. Amen" mean?

It means that we acknowledge that all kingly authority, power and glory belongs to God alone forever and so he is worthy of our obedience, love and service. It also means that if a human government or other authority commands us to disobey the Word of God, "We must obey God rather than men" (Acts 5:29).

These final phrases form a fitting conclusion to the prayer as a whole. We were taught to focus on God at the beginning of the prayer by focusing on his name. Here, we renew our focus on God after bringing our petitions to him by a focus on his kingdom, his power and his glory. Each of these—kingdom, power and glory—could be expounded in detail. But all three remind us of the ability of God to grant all our petitions in exactly the manner that is best for us. Nothing prevents God from protecting, forgiving and providing for us. He is all-powerful and in control. He is the sovereign Lord of history and the Creator of the heavens and the earth.

CONCLUSION

The Lord's Prayer is meant to shape our minds, our hearts and our characters. We are to be people of the prayer, people whose worldviews have been reshaped by the theology of this prayer. In the Lord's Prayer we have a view of God, a view of man, a picture of our need, a theology of grace, a pattern for the Christian life and eschatology (end times). Jesus is the master teacher who packs into one short passage an abundance of spiritual food and deep and profound wisdom for those who have the patience to linger over its riches and savour its delights.

Questions for reflection

1. What benefits come from committing the Lord's Prayer to memory?

2. In what ways should all of our prayers be structured like the Lord's Prayer?

3. On what basis can we call God "Our Father"?

4. If we cannot be forgiven without forgiving others, why is this not a case of us attaining salvation by good works (that is, by our acts of forgiving others)?

13

What is the mission of the church?

"The purpose of the church is to do what
no other entity on earth can do."

INTRODUCTION

We come now to the final section of the catechism: The Great Commission. As far as I know, no other Christian catechism ends with a section on the Great Commission. This is a novel approach, but one that is clearly consistent with the evangelical Protestant character of this catechism. This part of the catechism addresses the question of the purpose of the church of Jesus Christ. It answers the question: "What is the mission of the church?"

Today there is a great deal of confusion about the mission of the church. Is it evangelism or social action or both? If both, is one a higher priority than the other? Are they equal? Is the mission of the church to save souls or to improve society? Are we building the kingdom or witnessing to the kingdom? Every Christian needs to be clear about the answers to these questions if the local church is to be effective in carrying out the mission Jesus Christ has given to his church.

154 THE FAITH ONCE DELIVERED

From the beginnings of Evangelicalism in the great revivals of the eighteenth century in Great Britain and North America, and even in the predecessor movements of Pietism in continental Europe and Puritanism in England, there was little confusion about the mission of the church. Both the conversion of sinners and the revitalization of the church were considered to be the mission of the church and the particular focus and calling of evangelicals. From 1800 to 1900, the world missionary movement was the focus of Evangelicalism, and the central element was clearly the preaching of the gospel to the nations.

Along with the preaching the gospel of sin and salvation and bringing sinners to Christ, there has also been, during the entire history of Evangelicalism, an emphasis on good works of mercy and compassion. This resulted in a great deal of social improvement. For example, the missionaries in Africa built schools and hospitals to meet the needs of those who were converted and as a means of converting others as well. The abolition of slavery in the British Empire in the nineteenth century was a direct result of the Evangelical revivals of the eighteenth century. The plethora of social reform movements in Victorian England grew out of the changed lives of people affected by evangelical renewal movements. The same was true across most of the English-speaking world. Evangelicalism focused on changing lives, and the result of changed lives was a changed society.

But something changed in the late twentieth century in the way evangelicals began to think about the mission of the church. The key moment was the Lausanne Congress on World Evangelization in 1973, which was organized by the Billy Graham Evangelistic Association. It brought together missionaries, evangelists, pastors and mission leaders from all over the world. In order to understand what happened, a little history is in order.

In the nineteenth century, the Protestant churches of the world, led by the English-speaking churches in Great Britain, the United States, Canada and Australia, launched the greatest movement of missions in history. Millions of people in Africa, Asia, India and South America are Christians today because of the worldwide missionary movement that began then. William Carey went to India in 1793 and waited seven years for his first convert. He persevered in the work and has become known as "the father of modern missions."

Out of the nineteenth-century focus on world missions in Protestantism came a desire for missionaries to cooperate across denominational lines and the modern ecumenical movement was born. The World Council of Churches was formed in 1948 out of two organizations that were essentially focused on missions. It quickly lost its vision for evangelism and adopted heretical liberal theology and socialist politics. By the 1960s it was dominated by Marxist-inspired Liberation Theology and was totally focused on social improvement.

It even went so far as to reject evangelism, and many liberal Protestant denominations stopped sending out missionaries altogether.

After this loss of the vision for world evangelization by the liberal World Council of Churches, the original missionary focus of nineteenth-century Protestantism was picked up in a movement of evangelicals that came into view in 1966 in a Congress on World Evangelization held in Berlin and organized by the Billy Graham Evangelistic Association. In 1973, a similar congress was held in Lausanne, Switzerland, and the Lausanne Movement was born.

At the Lausanne Congress in 1973, the question of the elevation of social action to the same level of importance as evangelism became a point of contention in Evangelicalism. Social action, which had previously been central to the World Council of Churches and its descent into liberal theology and socio-political activism, was pushed to the top of the agenda by a number of younger evangelical leaders from Latin America. They were concerned that Liberation Theology was threatening to make Evangelicalism irrelevant. Instead of offering a clear alternative to Liberation Theology, they thought the way to go was to emphasize social action and thus blur the difference between Liberation Theology and Evangelicalism.

Three views of the relationship between evangelism and social action were debated. The first view saw evangelism as the *mission* of the church and social action as the *fruit* of changed lives as a result of conversions. Both converts and missionaries do good works as part of their lives of faithful discipleship as a way to show love to their neighbours. This was the view that had been predominant in Evangelicalism since the eighteenth century and led to the reforms of the Victorian era. The second view saw evangelism as *passé* and felt the church should instead engage in socio-political activism in order to fight capitalism and bring about social equality in the hear and now. This socio-political agenda was held as the mission of the church by liberal theologians. The third view was a compromise view that saw evangelism and social action as *equally* part of the mission of the church, with one not more important than the other.

John R.W. Stott, one of the greatest Bible expositors of the twentieth century, was chairman of the committee charged with drafting the final statement to be issued at the Lausanne Congress reflecting the mind of the participants. Later Stott described, in his highly influential book *Christian Mission in the Modern World*,[1] how his thinking changed as a result of the debates at the Lausanne Congress. He admits that he previously believed, as he said in Berlin in 1966, the mission of the church was the proclamation

---

[1] John R.W. Stott, *Christian Mission in the Modern World* (Downers Grove: InterVarsity Press, 2008, [1st ed 1975]).

of the gospel and the conversion of sinners; in other words, it is evangelism and missions. This was the historic view that came under attack in the liberal Protestant denominations in the late nineteenth and early twentieth centuries. This historic view was challenged in 1973 at the Lausanne Congress and Stott wrote that he had changed his mind and now thought "the actual Commission itself must be understood to include social as well as evangelistic responsibility."[2] He explained that there are three main views among evangelicals: (1) social action as a *means* to evangelism; (2) social action as a *manifestation* of evangelism; and (3) social actions as a *partner* of evangelism. Stott said he had moved from the second position to the third position. He elaborated about the relationship between evangelism and social action:

> Each stands on its own feet in its own right alongside the other. Neither is a means to the other, or even a manifestation of the other. For each is an end in itself.[3]

What are we to make of all this? This may seem like a small change, but it had gigantic implications for the church and her mission. How do we know what major changes could come from such a seemingly minor change in doctrine? Well, we do not have to rely on mere speculation; after all, we have the actual history of the decline of missions and evangelism among mainline Protestant denominations in the past century to instruct us. History shows that when denominations lose their gospel convictions, social activism soon takes the place of evangelism.

Here is a summary of the steps by which nineteenth-century evangelicals went from being the churches that powered the greatest missionary outreach in history to being dead, liberal churches, full of heresy and obstacles to the mission of the church.

1. Social action is introduced into the definition of the church's mission alongside evangelism.
2. It is claimed that the mission of the church is being carried out when either one of social action or evangelism is being done.
3. Social action is gradually emphasized more and more at the expense of evangelism. More and more resources of the church are gradually diverted from evangelistic and church-planting ministries toward various types of social action. The church gets more and more involved in left-wing politics.
4. Evangelism is downplayed and disparaged as "colonialism," "cultural imperialism" or "proselytizing." Inter-faith dialogue is stressed instead

---

[2] Stott, *Christian Mission in the Modern World*, 37.
[3] Stott, *Christian Mission in the Modern World*, 43.

of preaching for conversion.

5. Increasingly the church does almost nothing but social action, but if challenged, continues to give lip service to the need for evangelism.
6. Finally, the church comes right out and denies that evangelism is part of the church's mission. At this point, social action becomes the entire mission of the church.

The question, in light of the history of Protestantism in the nineteenth and twentieth centuries, is what is the future of Evangelicalism? Will it go liberal? Will it remain faithful to the gospel and the mission of the church? Will it split again as it did between 1890 and 1930? This catechism deals with this issue and helps clarify the theological implications of the view that the mission of the church should be expanded to include social action as well as evangelism. We will now examine what the Scriptures teach regarding the mission of the church.

I. THE DEFINITENESS OF THE CHURCH'S MISSION

The mission of the church is not something we get to make up, change or improve. We go to Scripture for answers.

QUESTION 78: Why has God left the church on earth rather than taking believers to heaven immediately?

He has given his church a specific mission to carry out in the power of the Spirit.

The mission is not vague, evolving or subject to our attempts to *improve* it. It is definite. So, what is it, exactly?

QUESTION 79: What is that mission?

Jesus gave it to us when he said: "All authority in heaven and on earth has been given to me. Go therefore and make disciples of all nations, baptizing them in the name of the Father and of the Son and of the Holy Spirit, teaching them to observe all that I have commanded you. And behold, I am with you always, to the end of the age" (Matthew 28:18–20).

Jesus left his disciples with a clear mission: to make disciples and teach them. The Great Commission of our Lord is the definition of the mission of the church, and it is very precise.

Confronted with Question 78, which asks why believers are not taken directly to heaven once they are saved, many people would be hard pressed to come up with an answer. Some might answer this question with a reference to personal sanctification and the need for us to grow in grace. Others might think that God is just nice to let us enjoy life a little before we die—although if we are going to heaven it would seem that the sooner we get there, the sooner the enjoyment will start! Perhaps this answer is connected to the problematic view many people have that God somehow *owes* us a happy, prosperous, healthy, trouble-free life. Many Christians seem utterly astonished when the normal trials and tribulations of life strike us personally. If we saw the purpose of life in terms of *God's mission*, rather than our personal happiness, maybe we would be less surprised and more ready to trust God when the storms of life inevitably come.

It seems clear that we would have a healthier and more realistic perspective on the ups and downs of life if we realized the reason we are on this earth between conversion and death is not for our own sake, but for the sake of God's mission. We need to become theocentric in our thinking, as we saw in our discussion of the Lord's Prayer. Ironically, this is the way to true happiness. The less we fixate on ourselves and the more we live for God and others, the happier we are. However, that is a by-product, the main *focus* of our lives should be the Great Commission.

As the answer to Question 79 tells us, the mission of the church is not whatever *we* want it to be. It is not whatever the church votes in as its own choice of mission statements. It does not change over time, and it is no different in the twenty-first century than it was in the first century or the eighteenth century. The mission of the church is specific, definite and permanent. It is determined by Jesus Christ, the Lord of the Church, and given directly by him to his apostles, who represent all of us who are part of the church. We do not really need to speculate or deliberate about what it should be—we can read it in Matthew 28:18–20.

II. THE NATURE OF THE CHURCH'S MISSION

QUESTION 80: What is the essence of this mission?

It is to make disciples of all nations.

QUESTION 81: What does it mean to make disciples?

Making disciples has two parts: evangelism and teaching.

These are the two main actions commanded by Jesus in Matthew 28:18–20. "Go" is not the main verb; it means "in your going" or "as you go" make disciples and teach them. Jesus assumed they would not be staying on the mountaintop forever! So as they go back to their daily lives—wherever they go from there—they are to be about the business of disciple-making.

QUESTION 82: What is evangelism?

It is preaching the gospel and baptizing all those who repent and believe the gospel.

QUESTION 83: What do we mean by teaching?

It means instructing converts in the Scriptures and the basics of the Christian faith so that they can understand sermons in church and read the Bible profitably for their own spiritual growth.

The debate over the relationship between evangelism and social action in contemporary Evangelicalism is a tragedy for two reasons. One, it detracts from what should be the main purpose of the church: preaching the gospel. Second, it repeats the mistakes of the rise of liberal theology and the social gospel in the late nineteenth and early twentieth centuries. For several centuries before that point, Evangelicals had understood that social action—caring for the poor and needy—was part of the "all things" that new converts were to be taught. Following the example of Jesus, who had compassion on the sick and the weak, we are to imitate his love for neighbour and obey the Great Commandment by feeding the hungry, healing the sick and caring for widows and orphans. All this is part of the life of discipleship to which all converts are called, and it is the business of the church to teach this fact. But social action is just one of many things disciples are called to do as part of what it means to follow Jesus. We are also called to live lives of personal holiness, worship regularly in church, use our spiritual gifts for the building up of the body of Christ, maintain Christian unity and peace within the fellowship and so on. Social action ought not to be lifted out of the matrix of the Christian life of discipleship and made into the one thing necessary, as it so often has been in liberal Protestantism. Following Jesus *includes* caring for the poor, but it cannot be reduced to nothing but that one thing. This error is seen in liberal churches where people are enmeshed in lives of sexual immorality and idolatry, but think they are highly virtuous and above reproach because of their commitment to left-wing politics. Allowing evangelism to be sidelined by social action hurts people, cripples the church and stifles the moving of the Spirit.

The mission is to make disciples—that is it, that is all the church has to do. If the church does this one thing effectively, continuously, with a single-minded focus, then God will be glorified, the church will be blessed and—amazingly—the society in which the church is located will be improved as the salt of the Christian community preserves it from self-destruction and makes it more humane and less evil. The more true disciples are made, the more positive influence they have on society.

This is the tragedy of theological liberalism: It neglects the one thing that only the church can do in order to try and take over what God has assigned to civil government—and as a result, society as a whole suffers. It is ironic, is it not? When the church neglects to make disciples, the number of born-again Christians declines and society suffers as a result. You may have heard the oft-quoted saying "He is too heavenly minded to be of any earthly good." But to fail to be heavenly minded is to fail on both counts: in the life here-after and in the here and now. Born-again Christians are both heavenly minded and of a great deal of earthly good because they have had their lives changed by the power of the indwelling Holy Spirit. When the church is not heavenly minded enough, it becomes of no earthly good because it is not converting people and making them into disciples of Jesus.

If the church as the church fails to feed the hungry or clothe the naked or heal the sick, there is always the chance the government or a secular charity or decent citizens of no particular faith will jump in and do the job. And if this happens, chances are many church members will be found working side by side with non-Christians in the various charitable organizations in the community. But if the church does not make disciples, the Rotary Club will not do so, the government will not do so and non-Christians will not do so. No one will do it.

Making disciples is the *one thing* the church does that no other organiza-tion or movement or person on earth does. It is the one thing, above all else, that society needs the church to do, and it has been commanded di-rectly and clearly by the Lord of the church. It should not be hard to see that making disciples is the mission of the church. But what is included in making disciples? It has two parts: evangelism and teaching.

1. Evangelism

What exactly is evangelism? Evangelism is the first step in making disciples. It corresponds to the sacrament of baptism. To evangelize is to share the message of the good news of Jesus Christ with non-Christians and to invite them to repent of their sins and believe the gospel. When they do repent and believe, we are to guide them into baptism as a public testimony of their faith in Christ. By being baptized, they signal their decision to become Christians and join the church. Evangelism, then, is the entire process of witnessing to unbelievers, preaching the gospel, leading people to Christ, baptizing them and welcoming them into the church. Evangelism is getting people into the church and to the point where they are ready to start living the Christian life and growing in faith.

2. Teaching

What is teaching? Teaching goes on throughout a person's life. We are told that we are to teach new converts all the things Jesus has commanded us. So, we start naturally by teaching them the catechism. We teach them, for example, how to pray using the Lord's Prayer. We teach them how to grow in their faith by attending church, regular Bible reading and prayer, being accountable to other believers, supporting the ministry with tithes and offerings, prayers and ministry service. We teach them how to be Christian parents, how to witness to non-Christians and how to live lives of constant repentance and faith. The Lord's Supper is the sacrament of the Christian life, and we teach believers not only what Jesus taught but also how to feed on Christ themselves by making use of the means of grace.

CONCLUSION

QUESTION 84: What is Jesus's promise to us as we carry out the Great Commission?

The promise of Jesus our Lord is that he will be with us and never leave us alone (Hebrews 13:5). We need not do this work in our own strength because his Spirit empowers us (Ephesians 3:16).

Feeding the hungry and lobbying government are the kind of things we can do in our own strength. But making disciples involves changing the human heart, and that is beyond our power. We need supernatural power for supernatural work, and the mission of the church is supernatural work. This promise was not given to any other organization in the world, but only to the church of Jesus Christ. As has been stressed, the church is the only institution in society that does the work of making disciples; every other thing that churches do could, in principle, be done by some other organization. But disciple-making is the unique mission of the church, and only the church is equipped to do it.

How does Jesus keep this promise? How does he remain with us always, even to the end of the age, when his resurrected body is in heaven? The answer, of course, is that he is present with us through his Holy Spirit. As he told the disciples, it was better that he go away so that he could send his Spirit to indwell believers, guide the church and empower us in the mission Jesus has given us to carry out. Jesus is so concerned about the mission of the church that he is present through his Spirit indwelling, empowering and gifting the church for its work. We can cheerfully and confidently throw ourselves into the work of making disciples knowing that our Lord and Saviour Jesus Christ is with us and, ultimately, knowing that it is *his* work.

Questions for reflection

1. What was the precise point of disagreement at Lausanne Congress of 1973?

2. How exactly did John R.W. Stott change his mind after this event?

3. Was he right to do so, in your opinion? Why or why not?

4. This catechism is a tool for teaching converts to obey "all things" commanded by Jesus. What have you learned from it about what Jesus has commanded us to do?

The Westney Catechism

PART I
The Great Commandment—What God requires of us
QUESTIONS 1-3

QUESTION 1: What is the Great Commandment?

And [Jesus] said to him, "You shall love the Lord your God with all your heart and with all your soul and with all your mind. This is the great and first commandment. And a second is like it: You shall love your neighbor as yourself. On these two commandments depend all the Law and the Prophets" (Matthew 22:37–40).

QUESTION 2: Can we keep the Great Commandment?

No, we are poor, miserable sinners who constantly fail to love God perfectly as he deserves to be loved and who fail to love our neighbours as ourselves. "For all have sinned and fall short of the glory of God" (Romans 3:23).

QUESTION 3: Is there any hope for us?

Yes, but only if we believe in Jesus Christ as our only hope of salvation.

PART II
The Bible and the Apostles' Creed—Christian doctrine
QUESTIONS 4–27

QUESTION 4: What does it mean to believe in Jesus Christ?

It means to believe the message of the Bible because the Bible reveals Jesus Christ.

QUESTION 5: What is the Bible?

It is the inerrant and infallible Word of God written for our instruction. As Paul teaches Timothy, "All Scripture is breathed out by God and profitable for teaching, for reproof, for correction, and for training in righteousness, that the man of God may be complete, equipped for every good work" (2 Timothy 3:16–17).

QUESTION 6: What is the message of the Bible?

The message of the Bible is that Jesus Christ is the Son of God, the Son of Man and the Lord and Saviour of the world. The Old Testament consists of the writings of the prophets who foretold the coming of Jesus Christ, and the New Testament consists of the writings of the apostles who explain prophecies.

QUESTION 7: Is there a convenient and reliable way to sum up the biblical message?

Yes, the Apostles' Creed is a short summary of the biblical message that has been used in the church since the second century.

QUESTION 8: What does the Apostles' Creed say?

I believe in God, the Father almighty,
creator of heaven and earth.

I believe in Jesus Christ, God's only Son, our Lord,
who was conceived by the Holy Spirit,
born of the Virgin Mary,
suffered under Pontius Pilate,
was crucified, died, and was buried;
he descended to the dead.
On the third day he rose again;
he ascended into heaven,

he is seated at the right hand of the Father,
and he will come again to judge the living and the dead.

I believe in the Holy Spirit,
the holy catholic church,
the communion of saints,
the forgiveness of sins,
the resurrection of the body
and the life everlasting. Amen.

QUESTION 9: What does it mean to believe in the Creed?

It means to hold resolutely to the truth of these statements, which are a summary of the contents of the Holy Scriptures and the sole basis of my hope of eternal salvation.

QUESTION 10: Why is the Creed given in three articles?

Each article corresponds to one of the three persons of the Holy Trinity: God the Father, God the Son and God the Holy Spirit.

QUESTION 11: What does it mean to say that God is the Holy Trinity?

It means that God is three persons and one being, and therefore, he is one God. In his essence, God is beyond our human understanding, but we can be sure that we know him truly because he has revealed himself in history to Israel, in Holy Scripture and supremely and finally in Jesus Christ.

QUESTION 12: What does it mean to call God "Father"?

It means that God is not an impersonal force, but a real, living, loving person who made me and cares about me (Matthew 6:26).

QUESTION 13: What does it mean to call God the "almighty"?

It means that God is all-powerful and the sovereign Lord of the universe. Therefore he is able to watch over us and to guide all things by his providence. Nothing can snatch us out of his hand (John 10:28–30) and no power can separate us from the love of God that is in Christ Jesus (Romans 8:39).

QUESTION 14: What does it mean to call God the "creator of heaven and earth"?

It means that God is the creator of all things visible and invisible as taught in the Holy Scriptures (Genesis 1–2; Psalm 19:1–6; Isaiah 42:5). As creator, God has made man in his own image, as male and female (Genesis 1:26–27). Thus, we are blessed to have our loving, heavenly Father as our creator, and we are doubly blessed to be created in his image.

QUESTION 15: Who is Jesus Christ?

Jesus Christ is revealed by Scripture to be the fulfilment of Israel's messianic hope as the Son of Man and the Son of God, and also as the King of kings and Lord of lords. This means that he is the God-Man, one person, fully divine and fully human, the second person of the Trinity.

QUESTION 16: What does it mean when it says he was "conceived by the Holy Spirit"?

It means that his human body and soul were created by a miracle in which the Word took on human flesh by becoming incarnate in the man Jesus.

QUESTION 17: What is the significance of the virgin birth?

It means that the conception of Christ was a divine miracle, which makes Jesus both fully human, with a human mother, and fully divine, without a human father.

QUESTION 18: What is the significance of mentioning his suffering under Pontius Pilate?

This means that Jesus was a real, historical figure who died at a certain historical time during the period of the Roman Empire when Pilate was governor of Judea. This is not just a fictional story with a moral; it is history.

QUESTION 19: What is the significance of the phrase "was crucified, died and was buried"?

This emphasizes his substitutionary, propitiatory, atoning death on our behalf, which is the heart of the gospel (Romans 3:21–26).

QUESTION 20: What is the significance of the phrase "he descended to the dead"?

It means two things. First, it means that Jesus really died on the cross. Second, it means that Jesus experienced death for us so that we might escape it (Acts 2:27).

QUESTION 21: What is the significance of the phrase "On the third day he rose again"?

This refers to the glorious and triumphant resurrection of our Lord from the dead by which he triumphed over death, hell and the devil (Romans 8:38–39).

QUESTION 22: What is the significance of the phrases "he ascended into heaven, he is seated at the right hand of the Father"?

After his resurrection, Jesus ascended to heaven until the end of this age when he will return. He is now alive and ruling at the right hand of the Father (Acts 7:56).

QUESTION 23: What is the significance of the phrases "he will come again to judge the living and the dead"?

It means that one day Jesus Christ will return to this earth in the same way as his disciples saw him leave when he ascended into heaven. This time he will come as conquering king, rather than as the suffering servant (Acts 1:11; 1 Thessalonians 4:13–18; Revelation 19:11–21).

QUESTION 24: What does it mean to "believe in the Holy Spirit"?

It means that we believe that the Holy Spirit is fully divine, the third person of the Godhead. The Spirit fills and empowers us for service as we strive to do God's will (Acts 2:4; Romans 8:26–29; Galatians 5:16–18).

QUESTION 25: What does it mean to believe in "the holy catholic church, the communion of saints"?

The church is holy because all those who have put their trust in Jesus Christ have been made holy in him. The church is catholic because it includes all those who have put their trust in Jesus Christ whether they are on earth or in heaven. Each local church is a visible expression of the holy, catholic church.

QUESTION 26: What does it mean to believe in "the forgiveness of sins"?

It means that we put our complete trust in the atoning death of Jesus Christ as our only hope for the forgiveness of our sins (Ephesians 1:7).

QUESTION 27: What does it mean to believe in "the resurrection of the body and the life everlasting"?

It means to believe that on the day of judgement our bodies will be raised incorruptible and reunited with our souls so that in the new heavens and new earth we will live in glorified, resurrected bodies forever (Revelation 20:11–15; 21–22).

PART III
Baptism — Christian conversion
QUESTIONS 28–35

QUESTION 28: If you believe that you are a miserable sinner who has failed to love God and neighbour as you ought and you believe that all is contained in the Apostles' Creed, how do you actually become a Christian?

The Word of God promises that "if you confess with your mouth that Jesus is Lord and believe in your heart that God raised him from the dead, you will be saved" (Romans 10:9).

QUESTION 29: What does it mean to "confess with your mouth that Jesus is Lord"?

The apostle Peter tells us the answer to this question in Acts 2 when he says, "Repent and be baptized every one of you in the name of Jesus Christ for the forgiveness of your sins, and you will receive the gift of the Holy Spirit" (Acts 2:38).

QUESTION 30: What is baptism?

Baptism is one of the two ordinances or sacraments of the church, which we perform in obedience to the command of our Lord Jesus Christ. To be baptized is to be immersed in water by a minister of a Christian church in a public worship service on the basis of your personal and verbal confession of faith in Jesus Christ.

QUESTION 31: Who should be baptized?

Only those who have first, reached the age of accountability; second, repented of their sin; and, third, trusted Christ for salvation, are the proper subjects of baptism.

QUESTION 32: What does it mean to call baptism a "sacrament"?

A sacrament is an outward and visible sign of an inward, spiritual reality. In baptism, the outward sign is water (Acts 2:38) and the spiritual reality is the new birth or being "born again," as our Lord explained to Nicodemus (John 3:3–5). Thus, water baptism is a visible and outward sign of an inward and spiritual reality. When the Holy Spirit regenerates us, we repent and believe and, water baptism follows as a testimony to this spiritual reality (Acts 10:47).

QUESTION 33: Can grace be imparted through a sacrament apart from personal faith on the part of the recipient?

No, God does not choose to impart grace except through personal faith on the part of the recipient. Water baptism apart from personal faith is useless.

QUESTION 34: What does baptism signify?

The apostle Paul tells us that to go down under the water is to identify with Jesus Christ in his death and to come up from the water is to identify with Jesus Christ in his resurrection. Thus, baptism signifies our union with Christ through faith (Romans 6:1–5).

QUESTION 35: Does baptism signify anything else?

Yes, by virtue of being united to Christ, we also become part of his body the church. This is why we believe that believers' baptism is the prerequisite for local church membership (1 Corinthians 12:12–13).

PART IV
The Ten Commandments—Christian ethics
QUESTIONS 36–55

QUESTION 36: Can we know what is right and wrong?

Yes, we know right from wrong by discerning natural law by the light of conscience (Romans 1:18–32).

QUESTION 37: Why then do we sin by breaking the natural law and thus going against conscience?

We do so because we have inherited a corrupt nature from our first parents,

Adam and Eve, who fell into sin and came under the curse (Genesis 3).

QUESTION 38: Is conscience infallible?

No, one's conscience can become seared through repeatedly going against it so that it no longer works properly (Romans 1:28).

QUESTION 39: What happens when our conscience no longer works properly?

Three things result from being in such a dangerous spiritual condition: first, we no longer recognize the existence of God from his works; second, we can no longer perceive the natural law of God; and third, our conscience no longer accuses us of law-breaking when we sin.

QUESTION 40: What has God mercifully given to sinners in this dangerous spiritual conditon?

He has given to us the Ten Commandments, which are his moral law in his own words.

QUESTION 41: Why did God give us the Ten Commandments?

He gave us his law for three reasons: first, as a mirror in which we can see the danger of our true spiritual condition and be motivated to repent; second, as a republication of the natural law, so that we can know the basic laws that make life in community possible; and third, as a spur to a life of holiness, as we strive to be holy as God is holy (Leviticus 19:2).

QUESTION 42: Should we regard the Ten Commandments as a burden or as a blessing?

We should regard them as a gift of God's grace to poor sinners who need to hear God's command, in order to know clearly the difference between right and wrong and the way of holiness.

QUESTION 43: How do the Ten Commandments relate to the Great Commandment of Jesus?

The Great Commandment of our Lord Jesus Christ (Matthew 22:37–30) is a summary of the Ten Commandments (Exodus 20:1–17; Deuteronomy 5:1–21).

QUESTION 44: How are the Ten Commandments structured?

They are divided into two tablets: the first four contain our duty to God, and the last six contain our duty to our neighbour.

QUESTION 45: What are the Ten Commandments?

And God spoke all these words, saying, "I am the LORD your God, who brought you out of the land of Egypt, out of the house of slavery."
1. You shall have no other gods before me.
2. You shall not make for yourself a carved image, or any likeness of anything that is in heaven above, or that is in the earth beneath, or that is in the water under the earth. You shall not bow down to them or serve them, for I the LORD your God am a jealous God, visiting the iniquity of the fathers on the children to the third and the fourth generation of those who hate me, but showing steadfast love to thousands of those who love me and keep my commandments.
3. You shall not take the name of the LORD your God in vain, for the LORD will not hold him guiltless who takes his name in vain.
4. Remember the Sabbath day, to keep it holy. Six days you shall labor, and do all your work, but the seventh day is a Sabbath to the LORD your God. On it you shall not do any work, you, or your son, or your daughter, your male servant, or your female servant, or your livestock, or the sojourner who is within your gates. For in six days the LORD made heaven and earth, the sea, and all that is in them, and rested on the seventh day. Therefore the LORD blessed the Sabbath day and made it holy.
5. Honor your father and your mother, that your days may be long in the land that the LORD your God is giving you.
6. You shall not murder.
7. You shall not commit adultery.
8. You shall not steal.
9. You shall not bear false witness against your neighbor.
10. You shall not covet your neighbor's house; you shall not covet your neighbor's wife, or his male servant, or his female servant, or his ox, or his donkey, or anything that is your neighbor's (Exodus 20:1–17).

QUESTION 46: What does it mean to "have no other gods before me"?

It means that we must acknowledge that there is one and only one true God, the LORD God of Israel, and not to let anything else whatsoever be more important to us.

QUESTION 47: What does it mean to make "a carved image"?

It means to make an image of either the true God or a false god out of something physical and then to bow down to such images. We are to worship the LORD God alone.

QUESTION 48: What does it mean to "take the name of the LORD your God in vain"?

It means to use the name of God as a swear word or to invoke it carelessly.

QUESTION 49: What does it mean to "remember the Sabbath day, to keep it holy"?

It means to use it for worship, rest and spiritual activities that draw us closer to God.

QUESTION 50: What does it mean to "honor your father and your mother"?

It means that we must obey all authorities placed over us by God with respect and humility, beginning with our parents and including teachers, employers and human governments. We are not, however, to obey any human authority that orders us to break one of God's commandments (Acts 4:19–20). We also honour parents by caring for them when they become old or sick.

QUESTION 51: What does it mean to commit murder?

Murder is taking human life intentionally and unlawfully. This does not include capital punishment or killing in a just war, which are not unlawful. It does include abortion, infanticide, euthanasia, suicide and all forms of private killing for evil motives such as convenience, revenge, robbery or hatred.

QUESTION 52: What does it mean to commit adultery?

It means to break the marriage covenant and thereby to destroy the family. This commandment prohibits all forms of sexual activity outside of heterosexual, permanent, procreative marriage, including fornication, homosexuality, incest, bestiality, pornography and all other forms of sexual immorality.

QUESTION 53: What does it mean to steal?

It means to take anything that does not belong to us. We may steal in many ways, including outright robbery or theft, but also by failing to fulfil contracts and other obligations.

QUESTION 54: What does it mean to "bear false witness against your neighbor"?

It means to tell an untruth intended to harm another person. Our word should be our bond, and we must be honest in our words and dealings.

QUESTION 55: What does it mean to covet?

It means to lust after things that belong to our neighbour. We are to be content with what God has given us.

PART V
The Lord's Supper—Christian worship
QUESTIONS 56–63

QUESTION 56: What is the heart of Christian worship?

Worship includes many elements, including praise, confession and prayer. But the heart of Christian worship is the proclamation of the gospel by two means: the preaching of the Word and the celebration of the two ordinances or sacraments given by our Lord as visible signs of the gospel, namely, baptism and the Lord's Supper.

QUESTION 57: What is the Lord's Supper?

The Lord's Supper (also known as Communion or the Eucharist) is one of the two ordinances or sacraments of the church, which we perform in obedience to the command of our Lord Jesus Christ. In the Lord's Supper we eat the bread and drink of the cup as a celebration of thanksgiving for Christ's death, an experience of our union with him and as a proclamation of his death until he comes again.

QUESTION 58: When was the first Lord's Supper?

It took place on the night before Jesus was crucified, when Jesus commanded his disciples, "Do this in remembrance of me" (Luke 22:14–23; Matthew 26:26–29).

QUESTION 59: What is the significance of the bread?

Jesus took bread and broke it and said: "This is my body, which is given for you" (Luke 22:19).

QUESTION 60: What is the significance of the cup?

Jesus took the cup after supper saying: "Drink of it, all of you, for this is my blood of the covenant, which is poured out for many for the forgiveness of sins" (Matthew 26:27–28).

QUESTION 61: Is it just a memorial of a past event?

No, it is that and more. It is a remembrance of the death of Christ and the great love of God who sent his Son to die for us while we were still his enemies (Romans 5:8). However, since Christ is alive we can also expect him to meet us in the Supper and impart grace to us so that we can be strengthened for the Christian life.

QUESTION 62: What can we expect the risen Lord Jesus Christ to do when he meets us in the Lord's Supper through his Holy Spirit?

We can expect him to sanctify us by uniting us to him ever more closely. Specifically, we can expect three things: first, comfort in our afflictions, second, conviction of how we need to grow in grace, and third, strength to live the Christian life.

QUESTION 63: How does the Lord's Supper differ from baptism?

Baptism is the sacrament of the beginning of the Christian life, and we undergo it only once, whereas the Lord's Supper is the sacrament of the continuation of the Christian life, and we partake of it frequently for our spiritual benefit. Baptism is a picture of our regeneration by the Holy Spirit and justification by faith alone, whereas the Lord's Supper is a picture of our on-going sanctification and hope of resurrection.

PART VI
The Lord's Prayer—Christian spirituality
QUESTIONS 64–77

QUESTION 64: What is the Lord's Prayer?

It is the prayer our Lord Jesus taught his disciples to say (Matthew 6:9–13).

QUESTION 65: Are we to say it too?

Yes, we should commit it to memory and let it form the structure of prayers in both worship services and our private prayers. Saying it aloud in worship services reminds us of the proper content and structure of prayer. Reciting it can also give us comfort when we do not know how to pray in our own words due to discouragement, sickness or distress.

QUESTION 66: What does this prayer say?

"Our Father in heaven, hallowed be your name. Your kingdom come, your will be done, on earth as it is in heaven. Give us this day our daily bread, and forgive us our debts, as we also have forgiven our debtors. And lead us not into temptation, but deliver us from evil. For yours is the kingdom and the power and the glory, forever. Amen" (Matthew 6:9–13 alt).

QUESTION 67: How is this prayer structured?

It is divided into two parts with three petitions focused on the person of God, followed by three petitions focused on our bodily and spiritual needs.

QUESTION 68: What is the significance of this structure for our prayer life?

If we want to experience blessing, we ought first to focus our attention on God and his faithfulness before we bring our needs before him. This practice increases our faith in him.

QUESTION 69: Why does it begin with "Our Father in heaven"?

We begin by addressing God as "Our Father" because Jesus Christ is God's Son, and we have been adopted as sons of God by virtue of being in Christ. Therefore, God is our Father, and we can come to him as his beloved children with all our cares and burdens.

QUESTION 70: What does "hallowed be your name" mean?

It expresses our desire that God's name be lifted high and glorified. God's name stands for his person and character.

QUESTION 71: What does it mean to ask for God's kingdom to "come"?

It means that we are to look forward to the blessed appearing of our Lord and Saviour Jesus Christ, who will judge the world in righteousness and set up his glorious kingdom (Titus 2:13; Psalm 96).

QUESTION 72: What does it mean for God's "will to be done, on earth as it is in heaven"?

It means that we long for justice and for the righting of all wrongs and for God to put the world right.

QUESTION 73: What does it mean to ask God for our "daily bread"?

It means that we are to depend on and trust God for all our physical needs including food, shelter and clothing.

QUESTION 74: What does it mean to pray, "forgive us our debts, as we also have forgiven our debtors"?

It means that we ought to be ever-conscious of our sins and ready to confess them before our loving, heavenly Father so that we can be forgiven and so that all impediments to spiritual communion with him can be removed.

QUESTION 75: What is a sure sign of this spiritual communion with the Father?

If we have truly experienced forgiveness of our sins by our heavenly Father, we will be able and willing to extend forgiveness to those who have wronged us.

QUESTION 76: What does it mean to ask that we not be led "into temptation" but delivered "from evil"?

It means that we rely on God's protection as we journey through this dangerous world as pilgrims on our way to our heavenly home.

QUESTION 77: What does the conclusion of the prayer, "For yours is the kingdom and the power and the glory, forever. Amen" mean?

It means that we acknowledge that all kingly authority, power and glory belongs to God alone forever and so he is worthy of our obedience, love and service. It also means that if a human government or other authority commands us to disobey the Word of God, "We must obey God rather than men" (Acts 5:29).

PART VII
The Great Commission—The mission of the church
QUESTIONS 78-84

QUESTION 78: Why has God left the church on earth rather than taking believers to heaven immediately?

He has given his church a specific mission to carry out in the power of the Spirit.

QUESTION 79: What is that mission?

Jesus gave it to us when he said: "All authority in heaven and on earth has been given to me. Go therefore and make disciples of all nations, baptizing them in the name of the Father and of the Son and of the Holy Spirit, teaching them to observe all that I have commanded you. And behold, I am with you always, to the end of the age" (Matthew 28:18–20).

QUESTION 80: What is the essence of this mission?

It is to make disciples of all nations.

QUESTION 81: What does it mean to make disciples?

Making disciples has two parts: evangelism and teaching.

QUESTION 82: What is evangelism?

It is preaching the gospel and baptizing all those who repent and believe the gospel.

QUESTION 83: What do we mean by teaching?

It means instructing converts in the Scriptures and the basics of the Christian faith so that they can understand sermons in church and read the Bible profitably for their own spiritual growth.

QUESTION 84: What is Jesus's promise to us as we carry out the Great Commission?

The promise of Jesus our Lord is that he will be with us and never leave us alone (Hebrews 13:5). We need not do this work in our own strength because his Spirit empowers us (Ephesians 3:16).

Deo Optimo et Maximo Gloria
To God, best and greatest, be glory

press

www.joshuapress.com

www.ingramcontent.com/pod-product-compliance
Lightning Source LLC
Chambersburg PA
CBHW030049100426
42734CB00038B/848